Challenges of Meaning, Love and Success

Claus Böckmann

Pen Press

Other Books by Claus Böckmann

Success – A Different Measure (Raider, NY 2011)
A Loving Company (Pen Press 2011)
Soulful Living (Pen Press 2011)
Hope (Pen Press 2012)

See: **www.clausbockmannbooks.org**

About the Author

Claus Böckmann worked as an NLP master practitioner, a hypnotherapist and a healer for many years. In this capacity, he worked with people and their conscious/unconscious minds, helping them to heal themselves by finding a more positive perspective. He has also worked in IT and sales for more than a decade.

Drawing inspiration from his own experiences and from his observation of life, Claus brings a unique perspective to the issues of meaning, love and success. During his lifetime, Claus has successfully recovered from near-bankruptcy several times, changed both his country of residence and profession a few times, and has faced considerable private and professional pressures. All of these experiences have enabled him to develop a positive perspective of soul, kindness and compassion, and an increasing ability to let go of fear in life.

From his considerable personal experience, Claus knows about the struggle all of us may face in order to find meaning in life, as well as love and success. This book, *Challenges of Meaning, Love and Success*, offers a unique way of looking at these fundamental aspects of our life. Claus is available for public speaking, consultancy and training, teaching and healing.

CONTENTS

◈ INTRODUCTION ◈

Meaning, Love and Success are, in my experience, three of the most fundamental issues in life. We want to have a purpose, a sense of meaning. Those who do find it seem to smile more often, and feel at home in and within their life more easily. Philosophers have very often asked the question of "Why we are here?", but this book is not about philosophy. I believe love and success can both provide meaning for us. But while we very often talk about love, maybe while watching a romantic film, and admire those who seem to exude success, both mean many things to different people.

What can you expect from this book? Certainly not a recipe for finding meaning, love and success and living 'happily ever after'. While some books and many people appear to have very definite answers, I have found that whenever I seem to find an answer, more questions arise. I am wary of people and books that seem to have more answers than questions. No one else can determine what meaning, love and success signify to you, or how to find, express and achieve any of them.

But this book, dear reader, will give you ideas, concepts, and at the very least encouragement to think about what kind of meaning you might want to find for your life. It will give you vignettes in the form of little chapters, looking at what could and does provide meaning for people. I am a keen observer of life, and my own challenges, insights and experiences allow me to consider aspects of life that concern many of us. Love, for example, is an expression of ourselves, and we have to find this expression from within. We also observe it in the actors of life and their actions, both of which form our continuous story of life: friends, acquaintances, colleagues, politicians, or people we hear about. Love has many forms and subtleties. It is when we extend this energy to others that we create a better world for ourselves and truly begin to understand its nature.

The quest for success has been a part of our story since the beginning of mankind. We read of kings and noblemen, knights, inventors, writers and entrepreneurs in our history books. We are told from an early age that we live in a world of 'survival of the fittest', sometimes in very forward and open ways, and sometimes in ways that are hidden among other aspects of competition and one-upmanship. I have looked at success from many angles, and I hope this book will provide a wider view of what success can mean to us.

Having worked in the commercial world, as well as in the role of therapist and spiritual healer, I have asked questions about both aspects of life – the material and metaphysical. We all want success in terms of recognition, security and growth, although we might not always admit this and openly strive for and advocate success. Being in a relationship with someone special can provide joy and comfort, and with them we can share who we are and grow together. Both love and success can provide meaning, and the process of finding both in many ways allows us to develop divine qualities; to shift and change, and in doing so, contribute to a better world.

When we look at and live life from a material and soulful perspective, we develop and live a full life story. Meaning, love and success can be seen from both aspects – there is no either/or. This book has been written with the intention of sharing some views and aspects of life, meaning, love and success that can help the dear reader to think about them more deeply. When you dig deeper within, you will access greater security to pursue a path of meaning, love and success that is unique to you.

May I remind you that any insight, any form of meaning, any understanding of love will often be temporary. In our fast-paced world success can come and go in a blink too. What fascinates me is our personal – and at the same time, universal – story, as we share so many experiences, situations, feelings, thoughts and concepts. I want to thank you for reading my book, and for giving me the opportunity to share what I have found out, experienced and learned about meaning, love and success.

Enjoy the book!

◈ MEANING ◈

What is the meaning of life for each of us? While it does not seem to be an obvious question for many of us, we can see the absence of meaning in our lives in many ways. I have met both young and old(er) people alike who tell me how empty and shallow they feel their lives to be. Experiencing their lives as empty, often solely pursuing material success, popularity or wanting to 'fit in' at any cost, and failing to find true meaning, they choose to escape from the daily humdrum: drinking, drugs, excessive watching of television or being online all day – there are many ways to escape.

Interestingly, while many of us seem to complain about the wasting of resources, stressful lives, the lack of meaningful jobs and the emptiness of pursuing power, status and success, let alone love in a meaningful relationship, we still seem to play the very game we moan about. For a while all our worldly pursuits can provide meaning for us:

the courting *game* as adolescents; the job *game* of climbing the ladder as young adults; the security *game* when raising a family–with house and garden, a secure job, enjoying holidays and friends; or the escape *game* of television, pubs, overeating and partying to name but a few. Inevitably, though, we notice that youth, good looks or virility slowly disappear. We start to understand that influence and power are fickle at best, and the question of meaning pops up more often.

Some of us start to inquire into the meaning of life, perhaps when illness strikes or death is impending. We might face a loss of someone close, or lose something important to us, and this triggers our search for meaning. When faced with a potential loss of life – our own or that of someone close – we might realize how shallow our life has been. We are not ready to let go and die peacefully, or accept the loss of someone close to us with dignity while still mourning their passing. At these times in our life we might realize that our life has not provided us with meaning. We did not provide meaning to ourselves. I have learned that meaning is closely connected with the attitude we have towards life – both our own life and towards the world in general.

As the psychiatrist Viktor Frankl explained in his world-famous work *Man's Search for Meaning* (Random House (Rider), 2004, UK) about his experiences in a World War II concentration camp, when everything that we know and hold dear has been stripped away, the only thing that remains is "the last of human freedoms", i.e. the ability to "choose one's attitude in a given set of circumstances". In the existential theory of 'logotherapy' that Frankl lived by and began to develop through his experiences in the camp, it is the striving to find a meaning in one's life that is the primary and most powerful motivating force in our lives. Frankl believed that our lives have meaning even under the most desperate of circumstances, and further, that we have absolute freedom to find meaning in what we do and what we experience, or at least in the stand we take when faced with a situation of unchangeable suffering. Those who survived the camp, and those of us who are able to survive in our own lives no matter how impossible the circumstances seem, are able to do so because we choose our attitude; we create some form of meaning from the events. Nothing has an intrinsic meaning – it only has the meaning that we give to it. Acceptance of life from the soul, through an open heart, is therefore more than a passive resignation. It is, rather, an attitude towards life, an active engagement with it, a deep knowing.

In listening to many people, I have heard repeated complaints as to how awful the world in which we live is. War, greed and pollution; a lack of courtesy and patience; an astounding pace of life; a lack of opportunities for many of us: overall, a world of lack, of having to make do and toe the line, of adapting to what is given, without much opportunity to shape the world around us. While, on the one hand, we acknowledge the power of the internet and the influence of social networking, on the other, we do not see the active part we can play in the *game* of life. When I talk about acceptance as a fundamental part of change, I am seen as old-fashioned and not in tune with the pace of the modern world.

But acceptance is not about the passive condoning of human actions that cause hurt, pain and death. Far from it! It is an acknowledgement that such actions happen; that humans still have a capacity to engage in war, rape and the infliction of suffering on others, as well as on themselves. Acceptance enables us to not be annihilated by suffering. Acceptance, compassion and the courage to endure, and to help to create change, come from soul. When we choose a soulful perspective in each moment, we begin to influence and shift the world.

Nature

I was 12 years old. My best friend asked me whether I wanted to spend a long weekend with himself, his parents and their dog, camping somewhere in Germany in a heavily wooded area. I had always loved the woods, and my parents were happy to have a quiet weekend without me, so we went there. We arrived late on a Thursday afternoon, parked the caravan and erected the tent where my best friend and I were going to sleep for a few days. It was summer and the sun had been shining all day, with a few sprinkles of rain too. We were allowed to explore the surrounding woods, and off we went.

When entering the woods, just walking without talking, there was peace. Moisture, colours, warm sunshine, nothing but peace. Our senses were saturated, our minds serene. No talking was necessary. Just walking, and later on, back at the campsite, just being; sitting around the fire. Dark, green and mysterious woods were all around us. People were talking quietly, all seemingly aware of a sense of sacredness. The sun disappearing slowly, there was moisture in the air, along with the sounds of nature. Birds were singing; a brook nearby murmured with the gentle sound of water running. My overactive mind was at rest, my soul was at peace, all worries were gone. Nothing to achieve, nothing to do, but just to *be* – sitting around the fire, listening to the sounds, feeling the warmth of the flames and looking into the darkness of the woods. The darkness was reassuring, not threatening. I was at home in a way I had never experienced before in my life.

With this feeling of peace outside and inside, I delayed the time for sleep. There was time for that later. My best friend and I were not talking. We both felt the peace, the unity of everything, and there was no need for talking or thinking. There was just peace. I can still recall that feeling now, as if it never left me; as if it etched itself into my soul. Many a time later did I again feel peace in nature, just by walking, listening, watching and being. If I ever experience doubt about meaning and attempting to make sense of it all, I walk in nature. Walking there is a feast of healing. I go back to my roots. Nature contains meaning.

Doing and Being the Best We Can

Only few of us will ever be famous, rich or very influential. But we can shape our world by being and doing the best we can. One of the most important tasks on Earth is being a parent. As a parent we can and will make many mistakes. It is in hindsight only that we realize we could have been a different, better parent; we could have acted and behaved differently in many situations. But our children are resilient and they will not be traumatized that easily, just because we have made a few mistakes. Countless stories have shown how people have turned their lives around and contributed something of value to society, despite, or because of, the difficult upbringing they had. There are, of course, many examples of the opposite effect and I do not want to encourage indifference to good or bad parenting. But we can only ever be and do our best at the time.

By adopting an attitude of doing our best, we create meaning for our life; it personifies meaning: as a parent, businessman, artist or accountant; as a cleaner, gardener or nurse; as a teacher, programmer, singer or writer; as a therapist, sales rep or auditor; as a politician or in any other of the many human pursuits and jobs. By being and doing our best, we contribute towards a better world. If we want to be and do our best we need to be vigilant, though. When we observe and check on what we do and say; how we are and behave, we will find aspects of ourselves that we want to improve upon. When we have improved upon any behaviour, attitude, personality trait, value or belief, the new us will be the best and do the best for ourselves, our family, company and the world, and so the cycle of improvement goes on.

We can only ever do and be our best at any given time. In hindsight, we might think our best was not enough, but we did not know any better at that time. Of course, we can learn from our past. We can continually improve, thus making sure that our best is contributing to society even more now than before. We find meaning in, and create meaning by, always striving to do our best, whatever that may be. Some are more intelligent than us, taller or more handsome, more sporty or outgoing, or more influential and charismatic. How we can use our abilities to contribute to a better world, though, is often not considered or put into practice at all. I have met many people who have outstanding attributes, but were not concerned with using them to the best of their abilities. Some were driven by their fears, and, by not challenging them, denied themselves the opportunity to be tested in life altogether. They became cynical and gave up, somehow just trundling along. Others had a high opinion of themselves, only to find out that life was not as easy as they had thought it would be. Others still were not aware of their talents or could not think of a way to put them to good use.

Does it really matter what we do with our life, as long as we do the best we can; be the best we can, within whatever we do? With an attitude of wanting to be the best we can, we can relax into life, taking the opportunities that are presented to us each day, and will, over time, make the best of it. Yes, we might have to let go of some dreams, as they remain unfulfilled and allow illusions to be shattered. We certainly have to adapt our expectations, shift our thinking and most of all, make peace with life. But all the while, we can just be the best we can. Do and be the best you can in any pursuit, job, situation or challenge – whether life presents itself in positive or negative ways! Meaning can be to just be and do the best we can.

Friendship and Hospitality

Some years ago I had a great time with a female friend from Belgium. We met in a park, truly hit it off and communicated frequently. She invited me to her house in Belgium, so I took the Eurostar, had a very pleasant journey and arrived relaxed and looking forward to a few days of spending time together. Helen was outgoing and very loving.

Arriving at her town, I was picked up from the station. Being greeted like a hero, as someone very special, was one of the most heartwarming experiences in my life. I was made so very welcome. Words and actions to this effect abounded, from being shown my room to having breakfast together in a small café the next morning. The menu was explored lovingly; I had the feeling that we had all the time in the world, and as we walked around town, I took in the architecture and the beauty of it.

While walking and talking, I always felt her concern for my wellbeing. This was beyond love. Yes, love was present all the time, but what was most endearing was her concern for my wellbeing. Was I hungry? Did I feel comfortable? What did I want to do? I suppose some men (or women) might feel uncomfortable with this kind of attention. I just felt as if I were being made welcome. We were lovers, but we were friends too, and I knew she always made friends welcome in this way. I learnt a valuable lesson at that time. Meaning in life can just arise from making others feel welcome. This can be true friendship! To be concerned about the wellbeing of the other person, from the moment of meeting them and throughout the time spent together.

We can do that with our family, too. Our children might visit us on a regular basis and we can make sure they have some favourite things around them. We can talk about issues they are interested in. Our parents come to visit us, and in understanding their little habits, we can make sure we pay attention to them. Inviting our neighbour into our house for a coffee and chat, we show them how welcome they are, with our words, our smile and our body language. In doing so, we are saying "You are welcome to my house, and I truly value you as a human being." Making others feel welcome, whether in our house, in a difficult situation, or maybe in a chance encounter, we can bridge the differences in culture or colour of the skin. Some people are naturally good at making others feel welcome, but some of us, including myself, need to practise a bit more. It is well worth the effort because making others feel and be welcome – reaching out to them beyond the normal etiquette – can become, or provide, meaning in life. Simple, but not necessarily easy.

Ordinary Life

When I was a child I dreamt of possessing the strength and abilities of Superman. I imagine many young boys have had a similar dream. I felt powerless in a world where I had to follow rules, stick to timetables and be a good boy. By my observation, a life of stardom, of celebrity gossip, of being special in some way still holds an inordinate fascination for many of us.

While most of us think and feel we have to live so-called 'ordinary' lives, at the same time our focus is on the spectacular and extraordinary; on special events or shows – in short, everything that allows us to escape the ordinariness of life. Men may watch football and identify with 'their' team, in a league or against other nations. Many women follow – if you'll allow me to generalize and exaggerate here in order to make a point – fashion, celebrities, partying and gossip.

Might we miss the extraordinary that can be found in ordinary life, though, because our attention is on the *perceived* extraordinary; on everything that might take us away from this moment and what we are experiencing right now? When focusing on the now; on whatever is happening in our life right in the moment, when breathing more deeply and allowing peace and joy to surface, we can often – and quite unexpectedly – find that we see and feel something extraordinary within an ordinary situation.

The other day, while sitting in a café, I watched a young mother looking after her two toddlers – drinking in the joy and smile on her face and the exuberant joy of her youngsters. When walking around a lake recently, I loved to hear the wind and feel it ruffling through my hair, and looking out of my window now I can see trees dancing in the wind outside. Watching this I feel peace, enchantment, and the ordinary moment of being here, while being present to what is happening, changes into an extraordinary moment. Our life feels ordinary because we expect it to be so, and as we assume it is ordinary, we are anxious to escape this and the many more moments that can hold the promise of the extraordinary.

The other day, I was thinking about a dear friend and the difficulties he had been going through, and I felt my heart go out to him. I felt my heart wide open, expanding, and in that moment I felt blessed, peaceful and grateful for the feeling of love and friendship I have for my best friend; for how he has worked through his difficulties. I was also reassured about the toughness and perseverance of human beings and our ability to cope and adapt.

Ordinary life holds a miracle to be discovered. By being present to this, our ordinary life, instead of thinking about something more 'intriguing', we open up to the miracle of this moment. This moment can teach us; we can be reminded of our love within and our love for others, or we can understand something that eluded us before. With our attention on the now, we are able to see people more clearly, and we notice the small gestures of friendship and commitment we might otherwise miss when our attention is away from this moment. Ordinary life holds all the fascination we need. It nourishes our feelings and can even satisfy our need for distraction, as when observing and being present, we always discover something new.

It is when we focus on that which is presented as extraordinary – on the future, on the past and others, on events and shows, on all that distracts us from ourselves – that we miss out on the miracles we can see in ordinary life. Ordinary life fulfils our needs and curiosity when we allow ourselves to stay open to it; when we do not look to escape. We can find all in the small aspects of ordinary life: a beautiful sunset, a gentle breeze that moves the trees, a child smiling at her mother, a neighbour talking to an old lady in need. When we open our eyes to 'ordinary' life, we realize we can gain all the meaning we need from this very moment and there is no need to look anywhere else.

Common Sense and Miracles

Having lived in this world for more than five decades now, what I sorely miss is common sense. Common sense does not seem to be popular at all. Governments and people accrue debts, spending money they do not have. We indebt ourselves to the detriment of further generations; we pollute the Earth, as if it were a dead thing that does not need consideration. We seem to run around like fearful chickens, pursuing pleasure, material wealth, status and entertainment, instead of taking time to have a close look at our situation – as a nation or on a personal level. At the same time, we have also lost a sense of awe for nature and the universe, and do not expect miracles to happen on a daily basis.

With common sense applied we are able to stop and look at our situation without rose-tinted glasses.

When we stop to breathe and listen to ourselves; when we look at our life with a sense of reality, we will realize that we overspend and often rush to escape a deeper sense of responsibility. We will realize how empty and devoid of meaning our life so often feels. We might also realize that we have very unrealistic expectations. When talking to younger people, I have repeatedly been told that while life is a dross, everyone can become famous and strike it rich. Television shows and sensationalist reporting of people who have 'made it' can give us the idea and feeling that it could happen to any of us.

On the other hand, I also encounter people who have completely given up hope of a better life. They regard themselves as being realistic in adhering to the view that "The rich get richer while the poor get poorer", believing that a select few are successful and have it all, while most of us struggle to make ends meet. They seem to have lost a feeling of possibility; a sense of wonder in their life.

I see life as a fantastic show of potential miracles. These miracles become obvious to us when we first use common sense to look at our situation in life, and when we see clearly and have realistic expectations. It is a point where we clearly see the limits, but also the enormous potential in our lives. When, for example, we understand that we do have to work for a living; to show and muster patience and perseverance in order to develop a business; knowing that without our input into life the universe has nothing to work with and cannot respond. Sitting idly on our backside and expecting miracles to occur without our input is not very realistic.

But miracles do occur. It depends on our perspective as to whether we recognize them as such. Whether we want to change our jobs, heal ourselves as we allowed ourselves to become ill, or see, all of a sudden, something that defies rational explanations (miracle healings, sudden shifts in perception, a resolution to a situation that seemed beyond resolution): it is possible, when we believe and know it to be true from the depth of our heart. In our belief, trust and knowing deep from our heart; from a perspective of soul, we can truly see and feel our life shift. It changes for the better. When we start to work with such a belief, subconscious patterns will come up. They will tell us not to 'expect too much', or to 'be realistic'.

Over time, and with patient work, we let go of limiting beliefs and slowly go from belief to trust; to *knowing*. We develop a sense of divinity and start to see life as imbued with divine and sacred power. Rituals, meditation, contemplation or seeing beauty in nature help us to develop this sense of sacred power. We become aware of it when we care to look and observe deeply; when we truly listen to ourselves and others; when we first use common sense to see our life realistically, while at the same time remaining open to miracles to coming our way.

I will never forget the day when I was told I would be made redundant from my last job. I felt elated, and when I told my boss so, he was very much surprised. While I felt anxious in some respects, thinking about money and security, I also felt a new world of potential opening up to me. I received a decent payoff that allowed me to stay off work and write for some time. Interestingly, at the time of being made redundant I did not know and feel that I could and would write at all. But a sense of opportunity came into my life, and I was in awe of the potential lying ahead of me. Both common sense, and at the same time, a feeling of a life full of potential miracles and divinity, can provide deep meaning for our life.

Life Is Work

In a world that does not produce enough growth for everyone to have work, and where automation and efficiency is becoming increasingly important, work is gaining in significance for many people in the world now. Work provides security, as from it we earn income. It also provides the opportunity for learning and growth, as we can expand, learn new skills, gain new qualifications. Finally, work also is a place where we socialize and form friendships – a pint after work, meeting for a coffee, or a friendly chat during lunchtime. We learn to work in teams, to pull together for important projects, and to encourage each other, especially when steep sales targets need to be achieved. Work seems to provide the biggest meaning for most of us.

Work offers our main opportunity to test ourselves against life and develop divine/human qualities too – patience and perseverance; leadership and team spirit; coping with stress and becoming a kind and compassionate co-worker, as we have the opportunity to lend a sympathetic ear to someone in need. Work can provide huge meaning and purpose for most of us. Our education system is geared towards producing great employees who have learned to learn and to apply themselves. The question as to whether it truly equips us for life beyond work is a discussion for another time, though.

In our work life we can get lost, though, feeling stressed, alone and pressurized. Use of prescription medications for depression and other work-related issues is high in the western world. Most of us will be aware of how fickle a job can be, too. Companies are formed and grow to produce profit for shareholders and owners. If a company could do without personnel and still produce profits, it would still be set up. I have seen many people enormously stressed and dissatisfied in their jobs, who only continued because they "had to pay their bills". They constantly pushed themselves beyond their limits, thus stressing body, mind and emotions. Many good books and articles have been written about different approaches to work within a company (see also my book *A Loving Company*, Pen Press 2011), and we can only hope that with time our places of work will become friendlier, kinder and more loving.

While work will continue to provide huge meaning and purpose for people for many years to come, we are at the same time making our world more efficient, more productive and more automated. More people are seeking work in all countries of the world, but fewer new jobs are being created, while older people are being made redundant all the time. Human beings are replaced by technology, or have their workloads increased as the workforce is continually reduced. In a world aiming for ever-greater efficiency, the idea of jobs for everyone is becoming more of an exception and less of a rule. People with fewer skills, education and training will find it increasingly difficult to be employed in the long term. We all have to take time out to gain new qualifications, have a sabbatical and change direction. It is said that we change direction in our work life at least seven times now – a big change when compared to earlier times. My father worked as a miner all his life and took early retirement, whereas I have already worked as a civil servant, then gained my A Levels and university degree as a mature student before working as a translator and language teacher, then as a hypnotherapist complete with NLP and healing work, then as a sales rep and now as an author, while holding down a day job too!

In time work will provide less meaning for us, and especially for the next generation. It might be time to rethink our priorities, and see meaning in our life outside work too. As a parent or artist; as someone who helps our community; as someone who goes back into education and retrains themselves; as someone taking time off work to heal and change and find new inspiration – there are many ways to find meaning beyond work. To make that happen we all need to change our ways. In our rich western societies, we can surely find ways to finance sabbaticals and other avenues that will allow people to feel secure and confident so that they can contribute to life beyond work. Who needs weapons in a world growing together these days? The money spent on them can be redirected to better purposes now. Let us all think about how we can change our own attitudes and contribute to our communities in a way that lets us find meaning beyond work.

Being Present and Honest

Meaning comes in many ways, but Buddhists have a simple answer: be present! Presence in Buddhist terms means to be present to this moment; to be aware of our thoughts and feelings right now. As this can require constant vigilance, discipline and much focus, maybe presence can be seen in an even simpler way. Not everyone is willing and capable of being present in the Buddhist way, so let us just be open and present by not wanting to run away from life.

Instead of daydreaming and escaping into many different things, we can allow ourselves to just be aware of our life. Awareness in the sense that we face our problems and concerns, and that we acknowledge and work with any problems we might have and whatever our concerns are: our anger, frustration and reservations; our guilt and prejudices and perhaps our self-centredness and lack of concern for others. Thus we learn valuable lessons. We are present by being honest with ourselves and the world around us. Being honest about our shortcomings, we do not pretend. We might, for example, just be managing to deal with our own life, let alone help others, and we can acknowledge that is okay.

I would love to be a better version of myself by expressing and living divine qualities more often. However, instead of showing concern for others and being more helpful, compassionate and loving, often I am self-centred, and not thinking about others. While I think that I am not judgmental, I am mostly concerned with my own situation. It is my assumption that many of us are in the same boat. Knowing of our shortcomings, we can honestly admit and be present to them. This is a great start. No need to chastise ourselves – our compassion needs to extend to our own shortcomings too. As human beings we live similar stories of being self-centred for some or most of the time. Accepting this gently, we extend this acceptance to others. Not feeling guilty, we open up our divine capacity of compassion, kindness and patience for ourselves and others.

We can be present by not escaping. Keeping our eyes open and remembering to breathe more deeply, we observe what is happening around us. We become present to our feelings, good and bad, and we do not push them away. There is no need to become a Buddhist or use a certain method to be present. We simply commit to not escaping anymore – not into a fantasy of what could be, nor into the delusion of being a better person than we see. We are present and honest by just acknowledging who we are, and by being willing to face our issues in life. There can be meaning in not running away, and in not wishing that life would be different. We might struggle to accept the life we see around us, so let us acknowledge our struggle. In doing so, we bring a measure of honesty into our life. Meaning comes from not wanting to escape, and from living the life we have with acceptance.

Accepting our life, we can still change it. We create love and success for ourselves, albeit with an attitude of being real. We acknowledge that at present we might be depressed, lost in grief and unable to move forward, as we are lacking the ability and strength to do so. We allow ourselves to be gentle, though. Change will come, as it always does, even if we choose not to do anything. Our perceptions do change all the time. Time and experience do that to us. Being present in the now through being honest with ourselves helps us to be in life with an attitude of openness. Presence and openness form the basis for change. Simple, but not easy.

The Certainty of Change

We can derive meaning in life from the fact that life changes constantly. Knowing that whatever situation we are in, it will move forward and change over time, can give us great comfort. As angry and sad as we might be, for example when we lose a relative or our romantic relationships break apart, knowing that everything changes constantly can give us the certainty that we will overcome this situation too.

As our body changes from baby to young adult to middle and old age, losing its suppleness but also winning because we are becoming more comfortable with ourselves and making friends with the temple of our soul that is our body, our emotions change too. Being inexperienced, as we are at a younger age, we might fly into a rage easily or allow ourselves to be upset in other ways. With age, however, we might not belong to the 'in-crowd' anymore, but there is a good chance that we will become more relaxed, more kind and compassionate.

Our thinking changes too. We might cling to some concepts of success, prestige or power at our younger ages, but later on, many of us will often think gentler, kinder thoughts, having worked with forgiveness and letting go, as life has taught us as much. We start to learn to let go of incessant thinking, often in a negative way, and connect with more positive thoughts. As time goes by, life teaches us as we learn to develop a wider perspective. Religious, humanitarian or spiritual concepts can help us develop faith and trust.

Becoming more aware of who we are as we age, the certainty of change can provide deep meaning and comfort. "This too will pass" can become our motto when facing adverse situations. Life is testing us deeply, and we are asked to develop and express qualities that have hitherto been hidden, buried beneath the surface. Meaning stems from the fact that constant change helps us to master life more skilfully. Knowing change as a fact of life, we allow ourselves to become more easygoing and treat ourselves more gently. As change fosters learning and growth, we find meaning in that, and peace of mind becomes our friend.

As a child I wanted winter to pass more quickly, as the many months surrounded by snow felt like constant misery. But I learnt to let go of my emotional dependence on the weather. I realized I could not change it, but I could change my attitude.

Thus I learned to cherish the passing times of snow and cold, of sledding and building snowmen, and in hindsight I realize how much I was able to enjoy those long winters in the end. Knowing change as the only certainty in life allows me to derive deep meaning. My patience might be severely tested, or I might feel exhausted from working long hours. But looking back at my life, it has been overflowing with meaning. What we lose in body strength and suppleness, we gain in maturity, depth of thinking and spiritual peace. Do most of us not change for the better with time? This change for the better provides meaning for us.

The certainty of change can frighten some of us. We might attempt to hold on to our circumstances, particularly when they feel positive. We cling to our material achievements, to our prestige and way of life, especially if distractions and holidays or partying play a big part of it. We have achieved something, and do not want that to change at all. After all, do we not deserve it all, having worked hard for it? From this perspective the certainty of change can look intimidating and we fail to look for or provide meaning.

What we cling to, however, might elude us; the more we strive for it, the more it moves away. It might be better to let go of certain expectations. Welcoming change, though, does not necessarily mean we have to let go of all material aspects. We can keep what we have and contributed further to it – after all, we live in an abundant world. What can change though, is our attitude towards it. We enjoy our achievements, but they do not have to define us. Meaningful change is about becoming more willing to share, while at the same time accepting that we could also lose it all.

If the latter, we have had a great time and what we lose in material ways, we can win in experience, in ease of mind and internal peace. The certainty of change provides meaning for all of us in different ways. Look out for it and allow change to provide meaning for you, in your own personal way!

Beauty

Seeing and noticing beauty is a matter of choice. How can we see beauty on the outside, if there is not beauty within? The world mirrors our internal landscape, does it not? On the other hand, we do notice beauty on the outside too, reminding us of the beauty we are within. Meaning is derived from noticing beauty; from connecting with and cherishing it. Basking in beauty stirs our soul, and soulful living provides the deepest meaning.

Some of us choose to only see decay, ugliness and hatred. We might choose this perspective temporarily, until we have changed enough inside to see otherwise, but for a while we fail to recognize the beauty we are, and thus the beauty around us. As souls and human beings, we are love and beauty, but we may lose our perspective when times are tough. However, beauty never disappears. Just notice and pay attention to it again, dear reader! It can make your day, lift your spirit and serve to confirm your loving attitude and perspective.

Nature provides beauty. Lakes and mountains; trees starting to blossom or leaves turning to shades of autumn colours; a landscape covered in snow or a hot summer day when people enjoy themselves – all beauty; loving and relaxing. Nature is a reflection of beauty in the world, a mirror to the beauty inside ourselves and a reminder to cheer up and enjoy life. We do not just see beauty but hear, taste and smell it too. Wind rustling in trees, the sweet fragrance of blossom in spring and refreshing water from a mountain spring – we take in beauty with all our senses.

Beauty is an expression of man, too. From the paintings of Van Gogh, Monet or Picasso to the works of art of Michelangelo and Rodin, we are capable of expressing beauty in its many forms. Poems and sculptures; architecture and design; philosophy and wisdom – beauty has and will always be an expression of human life and endeavours. Choose to uplift yourself when you feel downhearted, recognize that you might have focused on the perceived 'ugliness' of our world, and strengthen yourself by focusing on natural and man-made beauty.

Beauty can also be observed in a toddler learning to walk and being totally enthusiastic about life – they remind us to connect with a love for life. Watch them and feel uplifted. We can find beauty in the radiant face of a young woman or the wrinkled body of a wise old man. Why is beauty so obvious in the very old and young? Maybe because in contemplating such individuals we feel closer to our heritage – a divine being in a human body, as life has not yet obscured, or is no longer obscuring, this connection. Babies and toddlers express beauty in their spontaneity and soulful eyes and their still-strong connection to the source of creation, whereas old people can radiate wisdom and serenity, being closer to death and living life again from a more soulful perspective.

Beauty is a fountain of meaning. Connect with it; let it nurture and motivate you. Beauty soothes our soul, while at the same time being an expression of soul life. Beauty in nature reminds us of beauty in life, reflecting beauty within. We start to see the sacredness of life, instead of just trees and water. When soul-inspired, we can see magic in nature. We can feel at home and healing happens. We start a process of healing each time we acknowledge our divine origin, and being in nature reminds us of where we came from. When soul-inspired we express our divine nature too, and we start to see it reflected in anything and anyone.

Beauty provides constant and deep meaning in life. We strengthen this meaning when we acknowledge, nurture and express beauty. Focus on ugliness and depravity and you confirm this as a potential within. Our world and society are not ugly – we make them so with our focus; our inner acknowledgment. With a perspective of love, we see, express and nurture beauty. We have choice. Beauty provides deep meaning in life. We create this meaning by seeking out and paying attention to beauty within and without. I suggest that we all care to see, confirm, admire and mirror beauty, so we all acknowledge and strengthen who we are: a soul expressing a human existence, and by acknowledging and confirming beauty we restore our soul perspective.

When we teach our children to see, acknowledge and express beauty we create meaning for them. When we show them how to seek out beauty, they are reminded of their origin. Encourage them to avoid drama, gossip and too much fear, and instead to focus on love and beauty. This is the deepest service we can offer them.

Pleasure and Addiction

Modern life offers plenty of distraction, pleasure and means of addiction. There are many of us who look to pleasure and addiction in their various forms to provide meaning in our lives. Some of us take such a path for a while, but others indulge in that way for most of their life.

We are affected and driven by a vast amount of stimuli, much of which are intended to be used to create a feeling of joy and happiness within. It is within the nature of any stimulus, though, to lose its effectiveness over time – therefore we tend to need more of it in order for us to feel the same 'uplift'. Stimulation can be sought via alcohol, sex or distractions of any sort, such as gossip and drama, TV and sport. When our level of satisfaction lessens, we might seek a stronger stimulus: bungee jumping, abseiling, traveling - the cycle never ends. Pleasure-seeking and fun, often mistaken for joy, can never be sustained and the gratification they provide is always temporal.

Pleasure and 'having fun' are often shallow, too, and distract us from experiencing a deeper level within. The 'pleasures' of binge drinking and spectator sports; of idle gossip and drama, seem to provide meaning to us for a while. In the end, though, we see it all for what it is – an escape from our fears and feelings of emptiness.

Pleasure is, of course, not a bad thing *per se*. We can and do enjoy eating and drinking, playing and dancing, the beauty of nature and the ecstasy of love. We pursue pleasurable activities as a search for meaning, and we do find meaning within pleasurable activities undertaken with family and friends. Being with family, forming friendships and belonging to social groups strengthen our responsibility for life. Many of us, though, come to a place where we want to look deeper than just chasing pleasurable experiences. Life's apparent pleasures, such as power, prestige and entertainment, lose their allure. When we start to feel an emptiness within, we seek an additional dimension. Consciously or unconsciously, we strive for a perspective of soul, looking for a deeper meaning that allows us to enhance and enrich our life, while tempering our desires. We have come to learn one of the fundamental lessons of living life with deeper meaning, derived from a soulful perspective: that less is more.

We might also try pleasing others. Pleasing others – as well as, for example, amassing as much money as possible – is always based in a desire for control. When we seek to please others, such as our parents, children, work colleagues or friends, we place our worth in their hands. We become dependent on their judgments. This is not a plea to be antisocial at all, just a reminder to be aware of our (often unconscious) motives. As we allow those judgments to influence us, we increasingly move away from living a soulful life, and in this way true meaning will escape us. In attempting to please others, we focus on their emotional wellbeing and disregard our own, and so in a way we negate the value of our own life. Some become so lost in pleasing others that they fail to work with their own inner process; one which helps them to recognize that the terrifying void within is nothing more than an illusion. In place of the illusion we can choose the wonderful, peaceful contentment, self-love and compassion of our core soul being.

Pleasure-seeking can, of course, lead to addiction in its many forms. Sex, work, and in many cases drugs, seem to offer an escape from ordinary life. Drugs alter our minds, or rather, they pull us out of our habitual perspective of reality. Both the habitual perspective (which may be depression at the chaos in our life), and the drug-altered perspective (perhaps the calm or ecstasy induced by some drugs), come from and exist within our mind. Our mind is equally capable of both states, so which is the more real? Indeed, is either of them actually 'real' at all? **The points of crisis in our lives are always gifts.** That is a rule that we come to understand at some stage in our life when we seek a more stable perspective that can provide deeper, long-term meaning.

In facing up to any addiction we learn the rule that "This too will pass." We begin to sense that pleasure-seeking and addictions are illusory, in that they do not provide true and long-term meaning. Ecstasy, and despair as an after-effect of it, are illusions; transitory, and when we recognize, acknowledge and work with that, they are shifting too. It is in the nature of life that everything that is born will die; that the transformation of energy, blossoming and decay are constant; that fear, pain and tragedy will pass, and that so, too, will moments of ecstasy and pleasure, and addictions.

In addictive circumstances we can come to a point where we slowly begin to listen to the voice of despair that is the travelling companion of addiction, and we begin to realize that there will never be enough drugs, money, or whatever it is to which we choose to cleave in order to feel safe and in control. There will never be enough of these things, not because their supply is running out (it seldom does), but because we begin to grow heartsick and body-sick – of dis-ease and of half-living a numbed, confused life.

So often, it is in the moment when we reach rock bottom – a place so cold and bleak, so dark and silent, so hopeless and beyond our ability to conceptualize our way out – that we are broken open by it. Only then can we begin to hear the pure, clear voice of our soul – the aspect of our being that feels only love for us. It is from that moment that we can begin to transcend our subjective reality; that we can begin to heal and live our life from the soul level. It is then that we leave our pursuit of pleasure and addiction and start looking for true meaning in our life. We begin to seek meaning that is achievable, joyful and simple, and which comes from a perspective of love instead of fear. This truer meaning takes different forms for different people, but often comes in the shape of a stronger appreciation for our life, our friends and the story we and others are living.

Over time we can come to a point in life where we can let go of rushing and enjoy the present moment more often. We start to find meaning in each moment. We drop the drama and gossip and focus on deeper, more meaningful conversations. We start seeing life as a process instead of a pursuit of pleasures, distractions and addictions. We can begin to recognize a process of discovery and learning, allowing the ever-present joy that lies beneath our mental and emotional clutter to surface. By removing the layers of mental and emotional clutter, our joy will unearth itself naturally. We might decide to help others and spend more time with people we love. Meaningful personal rituals, like enjoying tranquil music, colours and scents, can restore a measure of personal intimacy and joy, silence and being, and at least once in a while, become our true friends. Meaning can come in many forms. Over time, as we leave gratuitous pleasures, distractions and addictions behind, a new world of meaning can open up to us.

Life Is Learning

Can we ever refuse to learn? Even if we are determined not to learn – maybe by dropping out of school, or trying to ignore new developments like computers and phones – over time we cannot fail to see the world with different eyes. Just as we cannot fail to communicate, we cannot fail to learn either. As much as we might want to ignore life's ever-changing landscape, life teaches us all the time, albeit often indirectly. Some of us cling to the old and want to avoid new developments, as we might feel that they can threaten our internal peace. That may be true, but depending on our attitude towards it, we do learn and adjust in a world of change. Whether change happens openly or indirectly, we never stay the same throughout our story of life.

Life is learning indeed, and learning in all its forms may perhaps provide the strongest meaning for some of us. Learning never stops – we continue to gain knowledge, shift and change, as young people, adults and elderly people too. All learning; all knowledge provides meaning. Learning and knowledge in a materialistic sense provide jobs and security, and security gives us the opportunity to test ourselves in life; to contemplate and connect more deeply. Being homeless and hungry brings about learning and change too, but a more secure life will, of course, provide a better framework for change.

As a divine being on a human journey we have come here to grow in wisdom, compassion, peacefulness and kindness. These innate qualities are in all of us and need expression and extension. Therefore learning and change for the *sole* purpose of security, or perhaps manipulation of others and one-upmanship, will ultimately fail to provide lasting meaning – a meaning that guides us to become wiser, more accepting and less judgmental. Learning and change purely for materialistic gain only does not lead to true inner peace and joy. Curiosity, an eagerness to develop our mind and intellect and to accumulate knowledge, can and does provide meaning for us as human beings.

Learning with the heart provides the deepest meaning for us all, though. While we might have accumulated a vast body of knowledge, impressing others and distinguishing ourselves, we gain true respect with the knowledge in and of our heart. Heart-knowledge provides a deeper meaning, and while intellectual knowledge can lead to admiration and awe, only heart-knowledge leads to love. True meaning comes through being tried and tested and having to dig deep to find acceptance, forgiveness and compassion – those qualities that lead us to peace, humour and serenity. We gain knowledge in our heart when we see and experience the pitfalls of life. Learning for life is learning from and with the heart, not just accumulating facts.

We gain heart-knowledge by offering a listening heart and mind to others; by holding back sharp comments and judgments; by expressing love as well as acknowledging the reflection of our love in others; by treating others as we want to be treated, whether we are young, middle-aged or a centenarian. A learning with, from and through our heart provides the deepest meaning in terms of learning. As we strive for this kind of knowledge, we build the foundation for our divine journey within a human story. In doing so, and in seeing life and learning as a divine process, we can embrace our daily lessons with humour, humility and courage.

Service – Just Being There

Service provides meaning, and people who have lived a life of service inspire us. Mother Teresa is one great example who, in my opinion, is a true inspiration. However, seeing service as something big and special can make us feel inadequate, and this means we are looking at service in the wrong way. Service can be a simple act of just being there for someone in their hour of need.

Two of my dearest friends are true examples of service to me and others. I call them my adopted parents as they are a bit older, and a bit wiser, than me. I truly feel part of their family, even if only through the stories they share with me about their children and grandchildren.

Shirley and Bob have always been there for me. We met under interesting circumstances, and many years ago I turned to them when I was not able to make sense of something I had experienced. They helped me, in their uncomplicated way, and we have been friends for almost 20 years now. We might think our friends are special because they do something special for us. Most importantly, though, I learned that we serve, as friends, by just listening and asking questions. Friends are just there when we need them.

Each time I visit my friends I feel welcome. We share food and drink, and we talk. During my past difficulties they listened, and only imparted advice when asked to do so. They live in semi-sheltered accommodation now, and mentally handicapped, older and frailer people are among their neighbours.

They share kind and funny stories and I know they often lend a helping hand: a lift to town so that a frail old neighbour can shop, running an errand, or just talking to them on a sunny day, listening and joking about the simple things in their lives. This is true neighbourhood watch.

Shirley and Bob are a hub for their family, too: children, grandchildren, siblings and cousins all have a place in their hearts. Grandchildren come to share their stories, burdens and concerns over a meal, and advice is always available when needed. Someone dies or needs to go into a home and Shirley and Bob will lend a helping hand: selling a house, washing and mending clothes, finding the right home or talking to the authorities. Any job that needs doing and looks achievable is undertaken.

We can all be of service to friends, family and neighbours. In that way we truly inspire, providing a simple meaning and answer for life. Not a proclaimed service that is undertaken in order to look good to others – this being the forte of some 'do-gooders' – just the one act that is needed and necessary in any given situation. Service can be very simple indeed – and fulfilling. Service – just being there – provides deep meaning for our life. A smile for a stranger in the street; listening to the concerns of a neighbour; helping a friend with a move; letting people know that we are available when needed. Service is possible in so many simple ways.

Life Is Righteousness

Recently some Jehovah's Witnesses engaged me in a conversation, as they like to do. For some reason, these two lovely people struggled to instil in me fear about the end of the world, bless them. My idea of a compassionate, loving and non-righteous god who does not punish seemed to irritate them, and they appeared not to want to listen when it was my turn to reply. At the same time, their idea of a world awash in evil did not sit right with me. However, it is possible that I might have misunderstood their message completely. They seemed to believe that the world was coming to an end – if not now, then later – and only those with what they regarded as a righteous attitude would enter the kingdom of heaven.

I have encountered many religious people who seemed very righteous to me. In this and former discussions I stressed what I believed to be the common threads of all religions: compassion and unconditional love. However I often felt I was seen as someone who was deluded, or not to be trusted, as I did not agree with their chosen righteous attitudes of punishment and sin. While I have met very loving Christians, Muslims and Jews alike, a big chunk of religious followers still seem to hold strong, and what they believe to be righteous, religious beliefs. Many Christians, Hindus, Muslims and Jews, to name but a few religions, seem to follow a strong religious doctrine. They can indeed come across as very righteous – and taking into account the large number of followers that all religions have, it seems as if a big chunk of our world's population sees self-righteousness as a major source of meaning in their lives.

Righteousness does not just provide meaning to religious followers. In my twenties, when going back to school as a mature student, I had contact with people who adhered to strong communist principles, and they too seemed very righteous to me in their stubborn defence of their doctrine, as did those who adhered to a raw capitalist model for business and life. The communists stole from me, too. In more recent times, I have encountered self-proclaimed 'spiritual' people whom I felt took a very righteous stance. Following an esoteric doctrine, they professed to know how life 'really works'. Those not following or agreeing with their concepts seemed to be regarded as ignorant.

I suppose it is easier to follow a given and seemingly righteous model of the world and of life, and it provides security and solid meaning for many. Being open-minded, though, takes more effort. What is most difficult, but also most rewarding, is to listen openly to everyone and be willing and open to adjusting our attitude, worldview or concepts, if and when we encounter an idea, concept or person that shatters our 'knowing'. Do we not learn most in this way? We are all surely righteous, to a greater or lesser degree, if only in ways we have not yet consciously realized. Staying open to life and people helps us to shift and bring to the surface hidden concepts that do not serve us well anymore.

The question "Do you want to be right or happy?" is one of the most impactful pieces of wisdom I have come across. I have been fortunate in that whenever I was sure that I knew something, my confidence in knowing was often shattered, and long may that last. Is there not always more to learn, change and let go of, including a sense of righteousness within that we might not be aware of? In a way, we are all right until proven otherwise. We might feel right, as we have learnt the scriptures or have political, historical, esoteric or scientific knowledge. But where can we take the certainty from? History has shown, as our life does, that everything changes constantly – science, medicine, philosophy or spirituality – and we always come to new conclusions.

In feeling righteous we deny ourselves the opportunity to learn and expand. We also exclude many people from our hearts and minds, as we feel that they are wrong in believing in something different. Righteousness has formed the world we live in today. Ours is a competitive world in which we struggle to share and love; in which we defend our way of life, of thinking, living, feeling and believing against others. In a world with less or no rigid righteousness, we would live more peacefully with more acceptance of our neighbours; more learning, growth, mutual help and support. We would move forward together and solve our problems as friends and neighbours. Do we want to be right or happy?

Life as a Victim

Recently, a German friend told me about her 32-year-old son with whom she has not had much contact. She brought him up as a single mother and did the best she could, loving him dearly. Unfortunately her son has taken to drugs, having complained for years that he had to grow up without a father. Repeatedly, he has blamed his parents for his misery, and believes that his unhappiness with his familial situation was why he took to drugs. His mum believes that he regards himself as a victim of his upbringing, and feels that he developed an addictive personality because of it. He thinks he cannot change his situation.

As I learned many years ago, it is when we forgive our parents for their mistakes; when we let go of the role of a victim and take full responsibility for our lives, that we truly grow up. In a way, many of us play the victim. Who can truly say that they are, think and feel completely responsible for their life? Playing the victim can take many different forms. I used to share a house with two people from Lebanon who were Palestinians. They thought and felt that because of constant plotting against their people by the CIA, their country was not able to move forward.

Others feel victimized because of the colour of their skin or their social class, because they speak a different language or dialect, or because they have not been able to go to university. We might think we are too small or too ugly, and that our looks are barriers that prevent us getting ahead in life. We might believe that we live in the wrong part of the world, the wrong area in our country, that we have the wrong parents or that we lack the money to start a business – in short, there are plenty of reasons for seeing ourselves as victims. That is not to say that these factors do not influence our life, attitudes and beliefs, but does it mean we cannot move beyond them?

Seeing ourselves as victims can provide deep meaning for us. We seem to live an easier life which we do not have to take full responsibility for, as we believe someone or something else is responsible. Recently I was told by a 20-year-old woman that she was able to see through all the masquerades of human beings and felt that being so sensitive, intuitive and observant was a huge disadvantage in her life. She would have preferred to be ignorant, as she felt that "The ignorant are oblivious of many things", and that consequently, they live a less complicated life. That made me smile. In the world we see around us, some people are in control, influential, powerful and well-off. We see glamorous people – their clothes, money and cars. Pictures and stories in magazines are full of glamour. As a child I was often told that there are those who have it all while our family belonged to the have-nots, and for years I became increasingly aware of my childhood indoctrination; but I was later blessed to realize it was my responsibility to change my belief and attitude, and went through a long process of letting go.

The choices are many: we can define ourselves as victims of a dysfunctional family or of our social class, our cultural or religious heritage, our troubled psyche, or of our body if it does not match magazine images of airbrushed perfection. If we choose to see from this perspective, our eyes are blinkered. We lack the clear, panoramic vision that comes from a deeper perspective of soul. We fail to feel our soul energy, and are unable to be nurtured by our deepest self.

Likewise, when ill we can be tempted to blame our physical, cultural or social environment. We can blame our upbringing, the pain inflicted by our parents, our personality or genetic makeup – the latter two seemingly unable to be changed. That is not to say that these factors do not influence our life at all – they do to different degrees; but it is our task, according to my understanding, to move beyond them whenever and however possible.

Leading a toxic life in its many forms, for example, might be a result of toxic thinking, feelings, habits and beliefs: a thinking that clings to the superficial security of our social and cultural heritage, or the abuse of ourselves that makes us feel alive. Extreme feelings, such as outbursts of anger, can seem to provide a semblance of control and importance. Equally, we can cling to a religious or other belief that keeps us deeply entrenched in fear – a fear that is connected to a feeling of spiritual superiority and being different, which gives us a sense of importance. Once we understand that we are completely responsible for our life, we know we have choice as to how we regard these influencing factors. As a victim we might feel we are trapped by them, as a creator we know they might influence our life, but we can move beyond them in different ways.

We are neither defined by our place nor by our function in society. Nor are we the damaged victim of a dysfunctional family, or a superior being because we have been born into comfort and privilege. We may lament and resent and choose to be victimized by the shortcomings of an imperfect body; of a poverty-stricken or difficult childhood or of a heartbreaking and overlooked adulthood, but that is not who we are.

We are our divine self: the soul that sits calmly at the heart of all of these external attributes. We are the clear, quiet energy that operates always from love. We are the wisdom gained from our navigation through the world; the wisdom that finds, learns and expresses love, no matter if the straits through which we navigate are serene or storm-tossed. We are the soul that chooses love, because it is love.

As a victim we feel we cannot change, but we always have the choice to change even though right now we might lack the tools or understanding to do so. When we decide to change, change will come: fed by the wish to change our beliefs over time, different thoughts, new friends or newly-discovered tools for change will come. A drive for change is our soul pushing us and giving us clues in many ways: a sudden urge to live a different life, the feeling of being 'fed up' with our situation, or perhaps a friend giving us an honest assessment of ourselves.

With our soul in the driving seat, our ego becomes the agent for change and, aligned to our soul, takes action, propelling us forward. Through cleansing our toxic thinking, we often start cleansing our cells and our lifestyle. Accepting responsibility for our health happens on many levels: eating healthier food; observing our emotional wellbeing; working with our toxic thoughts. We might feel the urge to slow down our life and pay more attention, and we allow plenty of time for change. We may change our job or our country of residence, decide on a less hectic or superficial lifestyle, or choose to embrace nature and our stillness within.

One of the key lessons to teach our children is to take responsibility for and to fully own their behaviour, choices and decisions in life. There is no value in the victimhood that inexorably grows from the lesson of learning to blame everyone else: other family members, ex-lovers, employers, politicians, society, our culture or social class etc. We alone are responsible for living our lives honestly and lovingly from soul, and we need to help our children to understand the liberating power of taking responsibility for themselves and their lives.

(Keeping Up) Pretences

Have you ever met people who pretended to be someone or something else, and did everything to keep up a pretence to be that person, while privately they were very different? Keeping up a pretence requires a lot of energy. Some of us seem to derive meaning by keeping up such a pretence in order to appear the way we want to be seen by others.

A professor at a university I visited seemed to be such a person. He was a regular topic of conversation for his colleagues and students as they thought he had a much younger lover at home – I never found out if that was true, and it did not matter. What was interesting, though, was that all the gossip was conducted behind his back. He himself never talked about any private matter with any of his colleagues.

He was absent for several months because of illness, and came back, among other things, to look after my MA and exams. Wanting to be friendly while talking to him about an exam topic, I mentioned how pleased I was to see him back and healthy again. There was silence, a strange look on his face, and a really awkward moment. I felt I had to apologize and said I was sorry, as I did not want to offend him. He said I had done so now, and it would be better to focus on the matter in hand – my exams.

I have always struggled with the front some people seem to put up, feeling that they do not reveal themselves the way they truly are, and in this I have always had a feeling of a missed opportunity for an honest encounter and conversation. Honest and true communication – just being oneself – appear to be very old-fashioned values in our world, where appearances and reality seem to conflict with each other. We might think and feel that we will not be accepted the way we are, and thus keeping up a pretence can provide meaning to us. Our pretence can provide a form of identity. We might struggle to accept who we are, what our life is about and to accept life as it is, and pretending our life and ourselves are different offers an escape from our real personality and story, or a private world we rather hide then reveal to others.

Does the need to pretend not come from a fearful perspective? Rather than being honest, we fear repercussions, and so we pretend.

Low self-esteem, or perhaps a fear of inadequacy, makes us pretend, exacerbated by the fear that our pretences could collapse. I remember acutely how cool I wanted to be as a teenager. I pretended I did not care about certain issues, events, people and situations just to impress my mates, and girls too. I felt so unsure about myself. Such was my fear of humiliation, exposure and embarrassment that I chose to pretend. Connecting with that fear, I eroded my self-esteem further, until only my pretence of being 'cool' with everything helped me cope with life. Today I see the posturing of some young men in my local gym, and remembering how I was myself, it always makes me smile.

Being honest and truly oneself is not always easy. We risk rejection and humiliation, and when that happens we have to pick ourselves up and try again. At the same time, that is how we learn to truly accept ourselves, warts and all. When we face potential humiliation, embarrassment and rejection, life offers the opportunity to learn acceptance. We are fearful of being seen as ignorant, uncool or not on top of things. Our weakness might be exposed, and we do not like the image we present to others. In facing this fear, though, we can develop courage and learn to accept and love ourselves and our lives, just the way we are. It does take courage to simply be who we are. This courage pays off in the long run, though. We start to like and love ourselves, and in doing so, others too. No one is perfect. Loving ourselves and others is one of the most fundamental lessons in the school of life, including accepting and loving those aspects of ourselves that we do not like and might prefer to hide. A life of pretence is so much hard work, requiring so much hiding, deception and lies, and it causes more fear. Learning to accept and love ourselves takes much courage, as we often need to face unwelcome truths, but the benefits of being who we are outweighs any pretence.

Safety and Security

In the industrialized and developed world, many of us, dear reader, come into our lives in relative safety and security. We are safe from the potential rigours of nature as we usually live in a flat or house, and we have food. We feel secure, as we have the time and encouragement to learn, expand and become a better person, growing along with our developing body, mind and emotions. Many of us grow up with the expectation of being safe and secure for the rest of our lives. This can provide strong meaning, in addition to any other meaning we give to our life. But will that always be the case?

For us to become a better, a more selfless person, we might need to experience situations in which we do not feel safe and secure. We have often heard about people who were exposed to danger or tested to their limits – perhaps when climbing a mountain, operating in a war zone, taking part in an expedition or facing very unfamiliar, demanding surroundings and circumstances. Those circumstances brought out the possible best in them, as they showed endurance, creativity, perseverance or other physical, mental or emotional feats they did not know they were capable of. I remember a story of a woman who was able to lift a car and release her trapped child – something she would not have been capable of in normal circumstances.

While most of us do not need to seek or expose ourselves to such situations, a taste of being unsafe can do us good, as it calls upon the best in us. It could be a simple situation. We might be with friends in an unfamiliar area, maybe after a late night, and we need to be alert; to find courage and overcome our fears in order to get home safely. Or we might be walking in the countryside in fine weather and are then surprised by a huge downpour, strong winds, hail or snow, which forces us to think on our feet and decide whether we should seek shelter or walk home. Once out of familiar and safe territory, we are often asked to find courage and perseverance within.

Equally we can be faced with uncertainty; a lack of security as we lose our job or find we cannot continue in our current working situation. Stress, circumstances or illness force us to take a rest and reconsider our options. Being disillusioned with what we have done, we might decide to take a career break, go back into education to gain a new qualification, to look after a sick relative for a while, or seek a less demanding job. Having rushed through life, we take any of these or other options to find a greater meaning in life, and to restore our health and inner peace. Losing a job or feeling fed up are opportunities that come along for a reason: to rekindle our peace and joy in life, to expand our knowledge and understanding of the world or to develop qualities and traits which we feel we are lacking, or want to discover and express. It is the lack of relative security that provides our impetus to become an overall better and more selfless person.

We all deserve and need safety and security in our life as they provide steady meaning, but a lack of them can also provide meaning. A relative lack of safety and security (most of us in the western world will not starve, for instance) teaches us that we are safe beyond the material aspects of life. We learn to reconsider deeper parts of our being, like trust, belief and faith. In being deprived of some security we rediscover qualities we would otherwise not find. Too cosseted a life dulls our abilities, and does not provide enough stimuli to make us want to strive to become a better and more selfless and rounded person. A certain lack of safety and security keeps us sharp; on our toes, and we might develop the discipline to work on something new because we want to and not because we have to.

We might develop abilities we never thought we possessed. Being made redundant from my job in software sales was one of the best things that happened in my life. Within that circumstance, I felt encouraged to write, as I felt the urge from within. The lack of security and work routine added a further incentive, and I discovered an ability I did not think I possessed. Resting and just *being* gave me room for creativity. If safety and security provide too much of our meaning in life, we might fail to develop all of our abilities and not expand beyond a certain level.

What Others Think

As a teenager and a young man, I was obsessed with what other people thought about me. At that time, I derived meaning from other people's opinions about me. While I pretended not to care and to be cool, I was pleased when my father spoke highly of me to a neighbour, and excited when a friend told me that a girl was surely interested in me, as I had not noticed myself. It was later in life that I realized there are as many diverse opinions of me as there are people who know me.

Writing my books, and the resulting feedback, offer a perfect example of why we might want to let go of what others think of us. Some people told me that what I have written about is nothing new, whereas others were full of praise. Some find my style not engaging enough, too coarse or lacking in fluency, or found the topic boring as I was just repeating was has been said many times over the ages. It is true that nothing I say is new under the sun. Recently I read a book about patience. Being an impatient person myself, I already knew about the importance of patience in my life, but I cherished being reminded of patience through reading that book. It helped me to readjust my expectations, and to confirm and find my inner peace by observing patience in my life. This book, too, did not say anything that is new under the sun, but it reminded me of patience (as do other situations in life), and just at the right moment.

I assume all of us have gone through a phase in life when we were concerned about what others thought about us. There comes a time, though, when we relax into allowing others to think what they like about us; when we come to a point of self-acceptance. Is it not more important what we think about ourselves? Once we completely accept ourselves as we are, warts and all, the opinions of others lose their importance. Accepting ourselves, though, does not mean that we do not recognize our shortcomings, such as a lack of patience.

What can and does go along with acceptance is a willingness to want to become a better person, to discover, accept, embrace and improve on our shortcomings and thus grow in confidence.

Knowing this, and living in a manner of honest and responsible introspection and discovery, as well as working with a permanent process of change (for example, with true remorse concerning our bad thoughts and deeds), we develop a sense of humour, gentility and humility for ourselves and others. With this we are happy to let others think of us what they may. Their opinions are many, and often reveal more about them than about ourselves. We just move on and create a new meaning – accepting and loving ourselves, and because of that, working with a permanent process of becoming a better person.

Meaning by Being

We create meaning in life via concepts. Success, love, values, attitudes and beliefs – all these are concepts that help us make sense of the world and ourselves. But what about letting them go once in a while and just being? We have lists and methods of how to create love, success and meaning, but in using them we take facets of ourselves and turn them into concepts. Being part of and naturally expressed by the deeper aspects of spirit and soul (concepts again, of course), the energies of love, meaning and success do not always need concepts – they simply flow and are experienced as part of who we know ourselves to be.

Have we not come across people who never voice these kind of concepts? Some people – small children, for example – just live their lives, unaware of concepts concerning meaning. If we look at small children, before they have learned to use concepts, love flows from them naturally; success is just there as they apply themselves in a pure way, and their meaning is in just being. My sister is an example of a person who never ponders about concepts. Knowing her well, I realize that she hardly ever thinks about life in terms of concepts that could bring meaning into her life. She just lives her life, being helpful to many people in her circle of friends and family and being very kind and very committed (my concepts here, not hers), but she would never even think about that. She does not give a moment's thought to any concept that can give meaning to us – she just expresses who she is. She creates meaning for herself and others by just being and going about her life as well as she can.

Others, like myself, create and work with principles, ideas and attitudes to create meaning. With our mind and heart we want to establish what it means to experience a life in this world. We might not have come to a point of just being yet, or we are there and have concepts at the same time (they are not mutually exclusive). Sometimes, meaning might still elude us in some ways, or change over time. We might struggle with love, and success could be an infrequent guest. As intellectual people we need to make sense of it all. There is nothing wrong with that, though. We are all different, and there are diverse paths to becoming and recognizing who we already are. Some of us are just more naturally our true selves, as we might live from our intuition without asking too many questions. Others need to establish a firm idea as to what meaning they give to their life, either knowingly and openly or indirectly, subconsciously and under the surface of full and conscious understanding. Sometimes, though, it is great just to be, instead of wanting to find a concept or theory for everything.

Working With the Process of Life

Working with the process of life is about working with what we are presented with, which often is a representation of our inner life. Some of us are looking for answers outside ourselves; within other people, places or situations; or examining the success, influence, prestige and standing that others seem to have. But do we not give more meaning to our life when we stop looking on the outside, and instead listen within; when we are open to the moment and our present situation, however dismal it might look? We might just find peace – sometimes even bliss and excitement – and our inner life, as well as external circumstances and events, can become magical. Bliss and happiness are fleeting visitors, though, and more often we might encounter a shadow within. We have to face something we do not like about ourselves, and for a time we might suffer from depression and feel troubled and confused.

It is when we allow that to be that we successfully work with our demons and shadows, which are also aspects of a full life. Just as life displays a series of opposites – love and hate, good and bad – we allow ourselves to embrace all sides of ourselves, and working with our shadows; with life as it is, we come to know ourselves as light. Embracing all, we encourage our unconscious to surface. When we reflect, observe and embrace all we see inside and in the world too, we truly work with the process of life. Listening closely, asking for help, ceasing to try and just letting be, we encounter much less resistance in life. This can provide a strong sense of meaning.

Life is just here and now, and the process we work with is not difficult or complicated at all. There is no need to go anywhere, to achieve anything special, to wear certain clothes or to eat a special diet. Some time ago, a friend of mine told me that people who were not eating very consciously, who were overweight and indulged themselves, were not very spiritual. I did not know how to respond to that. I do not think that diet or any other special approach is needed for all of us, though. Special diets might work for some people, but others eat whatever they like and it makes no difference.

It is not a special job, a certain income, a house, being well-known or famous, or having influence that makes us or life special. Any life can feel and be special when we work with the process of life. There are differences, of course. Some people go hungry or live in war-torn areas, and both individually and as a global community we need to help wherever we can; but working with the process of life as it is will give us peace. All life is unique and wonderful, and we can truly feel blessed to live our life. Embracing challenges and accepting what life brings, we might not always get what we wish for, but certainly we will have ample opportunity to make ourselves a better and less selfish person, as challenges come to test us.

Meaning and Courage

Finding meaning in life takes courage, and we develop courage when we look for meaning. We might feel lost in life at some stage – perhaps for a long time – but by just being able to hang on and get going again, we show, express and develop courage, and our search can continue when we think we have found meaning, only to find it was unsatisfactory and temporary.

I have met a number of young people who feel lost and see their life as devoid of any meaning. A 22-year-old woman told me recently how lost she felt in her life. Seeing her life as awful, she regards people as shallow, unreal, uncaring and lacking in kindness. She shows true passion in her contempt for people and her belief in an awful world. I could have talked to her about beauty, service and love but recognized that she would not have listened at that stage, so all I could do was to listen to her. I trust meaning will come to her with time, as I do see passion and courage within her. Living a life without meaning; without a deeper sense of being, takes courage. Fear can set in very easily.

In such a situation – in feeling lost – we connect with trust, even if we do not do so knowingly. We may discover faith hitherto unknown, and trust and faith keep us going. What keeps us going in a situation like this, instead of ending it all? As is obvious in the young lady I spoke with, there is a passion for life and a deep search for meaning. It might come across as stubbornness, or sometimes as anger and aggression. "The world is hostile, so why should I care?" Not giving up and showing courage is a testimony to spiritual strength and a deep search for meaning. With courage, patience and tenacity we discover, embrace, express and develop divine qualities. As we are tested by adverse circumstances in life, we find meaning: developing such qualities *is* meaning.

The young lady might find meaning in the small daily occurrences in life, too. Not all of us engage with a deep and powerful meaning. Love, kindness, service, just being and doing our best, working with life as it comes and using our abilities to their best – these aspects provide meaning. Some will find meaning in religion, in their faith, their families, their work, their ethics, their learning and growth. Others might struggle for a long time. As a young person we might struggle to become part of a community – at work, for example, as jobs are not always easy to come by.

We find meaning by participating in life, and need the chance to do so. Life asks us for courage, and expressing life takes courage. We live in order to find meaning. In our search we need courage, and searching promotes courage, which is at the very source of life. As spirit with a soul, before entering a human life, we need courage, too – without it we would not live a life as divine beings on a human path. Courage and meaning are siblings, as are love and meaning. Love in its many forms can provide meaning, and love requires courage too.

Is There a Particular Way?

Do we find meaning by searching for a particular way of life? Some look at their daily horoscopes, some have a psychic friend and some are not concerned at all. They live their life without giving any further thought as to what the meaning of life might be. There is no particular way, but some ways seem easier than others. Choice and free will can be a blessing and a curse in this regard. We might be pleased or scared, as the choices can be liberating or confusing.

Life has the meaning we assign to it. Never do we assign wrong meaning, since any meaning we find and give stems from our conditions; our human and spiritual awareness, as well as the situations and challenges we have created and find ourselves in. Any meaning is the right one for that moment in time. We might follow a certain route, like finding pleasure or working hard; we get involved in projects; are busy as parents and in doing so, we might realize that there is meaning beyond that which we have assigned to our life right now.

With any meaning and purpose we attribute to life, we create and perpetuate a story. When working towards huge success in a job, for example, we often face enormous stress. Responsibility for people can wear us down, and we test ourselves in weighing business necessities against showing trust, kindness and compassion for our team. Often stress encourages us to look at our priorities in life, and we learn to be focused, disciplined and determined too. As a parent, we learn patience and how to stay calm when emotionally challenged.

We juggle different tasks – mothers in particular often do this, especially when also working in a job – and we learn to be responsible and to develop compassion and unconditional love. There is no particular way: there is our way and there is freedom of choice. With our free will we determine our own special way, and we find our unique meaning. In the knowledge of this, we can choose a way that moves us forward. Any way can move us forward, however, even if only through finding out that in fact it does not move us forward.

In our quest for meaning we become more aware and we observe, think and feel with our heart. We become ever more conscious to and by the response life is giving us. Unflattering feedback makes us think, and we change our behaviour, our attitude, values and beliefs. Life just asks us to apply ourselves to the best of our abilities. Over time our best gets better. Becoming more centred and relaxed, we learn, change and expand. Any path or story offers this potential once we look with open eyes. There is no particular way. Meaning is about choice, and in reflecting on our choices and responses we move ahead.

◈ Love ◈

Love: the strongest, most obvious and elusive of all feelings and expressions. Love should be easy, as indeed we are love, but often love is overshadowed by other feelings such as hate, intolerance or misgiving. We might feel we cannot express love as we do not feel it within us – love may be deeply buried inside. Moreover, we overshadow love by focusing on drama, gossip, negative news or righteousness. All this, along with our own shadow aspects and focusing on a perspective of fear, stifles the expression of love. Often our upbringing makes it more difficult to express and be the love we are, especially if tenderness, acceptance and sympathy were absent in our childhood. If we grew up in an emotionally detached, mind-driven household, devoid of true feelings or with abuse, constant judgments and criticism, we cannot be surprised that we are struggling now to lovingly express our true nature.

Love has many expressions. There is the sweet love between toddlers or young children, or the first love awakened in a hormonal way as a teenager, mostly expressed as lust. We feel love for our children and family, or perhaps a kind of unconditional love for mankind. Love is expressed through forgiveness and acceptance, despite deeply felt differences. Love can be difficult to disperse. When love arises in a young person, for example, but is not reciprocated by the other person, we might feel trapped within the pain of unrequited love. Love is the energy that makes the world go round. We often think it is money, prestige, power, cleverness or weapons. Not at all, as without love in our world, mankind would have already destroyed itself.

Money, as an expression of love, is an energy that needs to be circulated and used for good. Money and love both need to be sent into our world freely. Love is what we are, and seeing love in others reminds us of who we are. We are love in many shapes and forms. Love needs constant expression, and our human stories – billions of them, all special in their own right – offer an avenue through which to express love and know ourselves as love. At times love is the most natural and easy expression, and at other times, the most fabricated and difficult manifestation of who we are. Romantic books, songs, poetry and films, as well as psychoanalysis, fashion or advertising frequently deal with love – after all, our world revolves around love. Again we might think and feel that life is about jobs, disasters, gossip and events. All these things, though, are but an opportunity for love to be expressed. Some countries struggle with poverty and debts, and other countries search for ways to help – love in action. Disaster strikes and other countries send rescue teams – love in action. We express love in so many ways. Let us look at some of her expressions.

Compassion in the Making

Imagine you are attending a meeting of like-minded people, discussing certain topics. This is the group's first meeting, and everyone is to introduce themselves and talk about what is important to them. The first person, a middle-aged woman, introduces herself, saying she has a narcissistic tendency. "Oh God," you think, "what have I let myself in for? How long is this evening going to be?" You take an instant dislike to this person, and she does not stop talking. After a while you politely interrupt her, suggesting that given the time schedule it would be good for others to be able to talk as well. She smiles and hands over to others, but tends to barge in often, drawing attention to herself again.

Sitting there, observing, you feel your impatience and dislike and you wonder why you have come to this meeting. Then it hits you – or me, for it was me in this situation. I attended this meeting only twice, but was kindly reminded – and strongly so – that while I did not like that woman, she offered me the opportunity to connect with the compassion I am. I was given the opportunity to breathe and relax into the evening, and to refocus my soul-nature towards just being, and allowing my compassion to surface.

I felt compassion for myself, as I was about to judge. I had made myself impatient and taken a dislike to her, but I had compassion for her too, as she appeared to need so much attention and she tended to connect to others in a way that seemed to annoy them – as all present could see on each other's faces. In these and similar situations we can allow our compassion and our love to surface and be expressed. Knowing that we have reminded ourselves of who we are – love – we shift our perspective from fear to love at that very moment. What kind of fear, you might ask? The fear of being with the wrong people/person (yet everyone teaches/reminds us of who we are); of not receiving enough attention (we are asked to give attention to ourselves at that very moment) – in this regard any situation can and does teach us. It offers us the opportunity to express compassion. While I did not want to stay with this group, the experience taught me well and reminded me of my nature – love that does not ask for anything in return. These situations come along to allow us the expression of compassion, and to be at peace. We express and extend who we are in moments like this – to ourselves and others. In life, many situations provide that opportunity.

Unconditional Love

Unconditional love means imposing no conditions on the expression of our love. We love ourselves completely as we are. We might not like some parts of our body, our weight, our hair, looks or personality, but we have developed acceptance. Life gives us the opportunity to accept ourselves unconditionally. We are born, we age with time, and one day we will die.

We start to lose our fitness, our eyesight weakens and our hearing too, and we start to forget the odd things that we used to remember: we age. Do we completely love this aging body? Maybe we pay lip service only, and are secretly and subconsciously angered by our waning faculties and grieving for our disappearing beauty. While we might grieve for our lost youth, we can also let go of outdated and useless concepts, habits and beliefs. Life is a process of change – we can mourn and at the same time cherish the changes that come with time. When we accept our ephemeral state, we help ourselves to love unconditionally – we love all that has been, all that has gone and the time we have left. When we love ourselves unconditionally we start living unconditionally, leading to more awareness of this moment and enabling us to express greater joy and peace.

Once we love ourselves unconditionally, we can offer the same to others. We start to accept their flaws and their imperfections, while at the same time seeing their divine perfection. With unconditional love we pave the way to seeing divinity in others too, looking beyond their personality, culture and indoctrination; beyond their gender and sexual orientation; and beyond colour of skin – we come to accept and welcome all others as part of the human family. All of us are undertaking a divine journey in human form. While we might not like certain aspects in others, nevertheless we can cherish them as human beings. We can accept them unconditionally as fellow travellers, despite our potential misgivings. All of us do the best we can with the understanding and circumstances particular to us, and with what our life story has taught us. Knowing this we do not only accept, but cherish others for their courage to be and their constant work as human beings. In developing compassion, our judgments start to lessen, aversions become milder and we are willing to find, embrace and express unconditional love.

We have come here, though, to master personal love too. Unconditional love is our nature – we came from spirit to express it naturally, and eventually we will go back to spirit. We came here to find, learn about, embrace and express all forms of love. Universal love and personal love – the latter possibly messy and crazy; broken and sullied but also universal and graceful, and all expressed from a place of divinity. We stumble and slip; we practise and change, and we mess up. All this we do as we try for perfection, but we did not come here to become perfect.

We are perfect as divine souls and we want to find and express this perfection through our human form. We are gorgeous humans; flawed and fabulous, always reminding ourselves who we truly are. Unconditional love – what a heroic aim! All we need is to show up, though, doing our best and staying present as much as possible. No need for perfection as we shine and fall, laugh and cry, hurt and heal and then play again. We act, but forget that we do, and without an agenda our love becomes less conditional over time, until eventually it becomes our foremost nature. We just express who we are and allow others to do so too, and in their own unique way.

While on our divine journey in human form, we can still value others as human beings despite finding certain facets of their natures difficult to accept. We can accept them unconditionally as fellow travellers, even when we are aware of our prejudices lingering under the surface. We all do the best we can with what we have given to ourselves; with what our story in life has brought us through experience. Realizing this, we do not only accept but treasure others for their existence and their work at being human. With time we might become milder in our judgments and aversions, and our unconditional love in the making, with our willingness to express it despite our human misgivings, brings us peace within. We see beyond human flaws and look at the shining light others present to us; at the contrast they offer us in this world – for our learning and expansion.

Unconditional love is a process of becoming. We slip many times, and the conditions we impose on love and life are always surfacing. We practise, we change, and as we bring divine qualities from the inside out, they start to shine through more often. We slip, pick ourselves up and try again. We become better at expressing unconditional love until, with time, it becomes more second nature. We arrive at a junction where acting is forgotten and true being starts. Perhaps not noticing at first, others might look at us in astonishment as our light shines through so strongly. No reminder or effort is needed, since unconditional love comes naturally, and in becoming it, we embody unconditional love, having a natural empathy for others. Practising unconditional love has made us so, and in becoming this quality in life, we remind and encourage other to be so, too. With our peace and joy; our total acceptance, we act as a beacon to remind our fellow travellers, who are often not even aware of it. No intention as such is needed: we just are, and others have the choice of taking a lesson from us; to see us as an example of unconditional love. We are, and allow others to be too.

Forgiving

We truly love when we forgive. Forgiving may be the most difficult aspect of love. Forgiving is a process which can be a true labour of love. True forgiveness shows itself by result only: we find the person who has been forgiven loses importance to us and when forgiven there is no ill-feeling, anger or hate anymore. We forgave him, and he disappeared from our movie screen. We wish her well, but at the same time she has lost her former importance. Their behaviour, our misdeed, no longer matters.

It might take us years to be able to forgive, and the process has many stages. Most of us have our story, and here is mine as an example. I remember a person whom I felt had done me wrong, but at the same time my involvement in this story was not entirely positive either. Let me call this person Matthew. Matthew and I hurt each other badly – not on purpose as such, but because we did not know better at that time. I do not know whether he has forgiven me, and it does not matter. Overall, we need to forgive ourselves, as we trap ourselves with feelings of anger or hatred. We cannot influence the other person anyway, so if we find out that they have forgiven us, this can be a bonus. When they forgive us, they learn that it is for their benefit too, as they realize that the reward in forgiving is release from their own emotional prison.

Following the 'wrongdoing' by Matthew, I laboured for a few years, struggling for many nights with what had happened, what was done to me and what I myself had done. Feeling guilty and being angry with him, I worked with a process of healing – mentally first, then emotionally, and of course with ensuing physical repercussions as I released painful feelings. While in between I thought that I had made it, I came to recognize that there was more work to be done. Matthew stayed in touch, and each time I realized, gauging from my reaction towards his contact, that more needed to be done. Some friends called him a soulmate; others a nuisance, and their unsolicited advice did help in the process. As Matthew asked for financial help too, I also gained the opportunity to learn about generosity.

I feel this was the most important teaching for me and I had a perfect 'indirect' teacher. After a process of five years, I finally learned to forgive and let go – not just for Matthew but for everyone and everything in my life that required forgiveness, including myself. Often those most difficult, demanding and awkward situations and events provide the biggest lessons of soul. While it was not funny at the time, I have, want to, and do smile now. Matthew provided a lesson in love, helping me to open my heart wider and deeper, and I am very grateful for that.

Be Gentle With Yourself

Do you tell yourself off when you have made a 'mistake'? I certainly used to. On top of that, many years ago I also gloated on the odd occasion when seeing the misfortune of others. I did not like them, or myself, at that time. And we know better, do we not? We see others – politicians, actors, singers, colleagues and friends – making mistakes, and we may gloat, admonishing them in our mind and heart, or we might bask in their misfortune. At times all of us make decisions and take actions that do not lead to the desired results. We act in a certain way, a drama unfolds and we are bewildered. What has happened? We indulge in a negative internal dialogue, punishing ourselves with our thoughts and internal discourse. We create ill-feeling and confirm negative beliefs and attitudes concerning others and ourselves.

We can, however, choose to smile and accept our actions, our behaviour and our so-called 'mistakes'. Life is feedback, though. We said or did something that did not lead to a desired outcome and we encountered resistance – maybe a person who did not want to listen to us. It is easy to smile when life turns out well, but when truly loving ourselves we are able to be gentle in reaction, thought and attitude when life goes wrong. Maybe we are lagging behind in our schedule, but tomorrow is another day. A person did not want to cooperate, and we might have to work on our communication skills. Smile! We committed a faux pas and can laugh about it. Any 'mistake'; any difficult person or situation, is a gentle reminder for us to be gentle in reaction, thought, word and deed. We learn that there is always a different choice or behaviour. With each reminder to be gentle within difficulties we are advised to communicate and react differently next time. Be a gentle giant! You can abstain from judging others or yourself; you can choose to let go and be generous, gracious and gentle. Let it be, let them be, and know that tomorrow is another day.

We live in a world of judgments and harsh words. The media and situations at work or in competitive sports bear testimony to that. If we need to compete, let us do so with humour and gentility. Others can indeed be better, faster or stronger than us – or lag behind us, and it does not matter at all. Being gentle with ourselves and others, we set an example to follow. Each encounter and situation; each ill-advised action, is a reminder to be more gentle next time. Thus we set an example for the world to come, step by step, day by day, change by change. Our children will learn to stop judging, too, and learn gentility instead – in this way our world is truly going to change over time.

Letting Go

Letting go is a vital part of living, and of expressing and being love. Life teaches and presents us with opportunities to let go. We learn to let go for our own wellbeing, as well as that of other people involved. At the time of writing these lines I have not had contact with my son for eight years, five months and a few days. This is a long story and not to be told in this book at least, so allow me to just mention the fact. Like many other people in similar situations, I had to learn to let go, as I wanted to stay sane and continue to enjoy life.

Some people have lost loved ones and my heart goes out to them: loss can feel so inevitably final, like losing a son in a war, as a friend of mine has experienced. Maybe an illness has taken someone special away from us. Some fathers do not see their children because of an acrimonious divorce, and I can truly empathize with them. We can surely sympathize, but we never truly know how that feels unless we face the same situation ourselves. Like myself, many responsible fathers, whatever the marriage and breakup were like, want to see and be with their children. My son is a part of me. I have been told how much he looks, walks and thinks like me. His personality, so I am informed, is very similar to mine too. There has not been a day in all those long years that I have not thought about my son, and sense and feel him in my soul.

Following my marital separation, and the day I lost contact with him a year later, life went on. I got a better job, worked hard during the day and always paid a generous monthly maintenance, but sat in quietness each night for a few years, slowly coming to terms with it all. Over time I understood, admitted and embraced my shortcomings as a person and father – I am far from perfect. Like all of us, I am a work in progress and I am love in progress. But during that time I had to, and did, come to a point where I let go. I let go of the pain by working through a process of forgiveness, as well as the need for understanding, trusting that further insights will come with time. I needed to let go too, in order to move forward with my life so that I could change, learn, develop and truly live again. I had to let go for my son's sake as well. My grieving energy would have held him back. We both needed to move forward in our separate lives, to learn our individual lessons, to grow and change and fulfil our potential. It was not easy – letting go never is.

There comes a time when we learn this vital lesson in life. We let go of outmoded ideas and old grievances, or people who accompanied us on our path for a while, before parting from us through choice, necessity or circumstances, such as moving away. Loving life means letting go, and letting go of someone we truly love is the hardest lesson. There is a long process behind letting go. We might think we have done it one day, only to then realize that we have not done so at all. We move forward one step to fall back again by two. We struggle, as our mind, our heart and our hurt want to hold on; to keep it safe for later; to preserve a certain way of life, thinking, feeling and being. But there comes a time when we truly have to let go.

Love and Being Right

A few years ago, a German friend told me about a couple who seemed to have a wonderful marriage, still being besotted with each other after more than

30 years. When asked what their recipe for a long and successful marriage was, they said that it was letting go of wanting to be right, and letting the other be as they are at any given moment. Early in their relationship they had decided to forgo the certainty of being right when they thought the other person was wrong. They wanted to let their partner to come to their own conclusions instead.

That, as they said, had not always been easy. They did not want the other to get hurt emotionally, and telling them when they thought that they were wrong might have prevented that. I personally remember a great relationship with a hot-blooded lady, where we quarrelled through the day – through most days – and made up for it during the night. Thinking about how exhausting the resulting emotional turmoil was, I wonder how this relationship lasted for two years.

Hands up those who like to be wrong. Many a time I have seen couples stubbornly fighting over who is right, at the risk of losing their love and relationship. Wanting to be right, we often cause a great deal of stress and pain for both ourselves and our partners. Being right is a matter of perspective, is it not? We might think we know what is right, even for another person, but are we truly walking in their shoes? Even if we think they are wrong, they might need to walk along the 'path of wrong' for a while for them to realize what is right for them.

Often I realized that what I thought was right at some stage turned out to be wrong later on, or that it needed some change; some improvement.

At times it was a certain attitude I had, or a view I adhered to strongly, only to find out later that it was flawed in the first place. Often my view came from too narrow a perspective, and it was my path to learn. I went from wanting to be right to realizing that being right is temporary at best, as my perspective is always broadening with continued experience in life.

Wanting to be right is just not worth it. We might want to jump into a fight over who is right and wrong, but the question to ask is whether we want to right, or kind and happy. Being right might inflate our ego, but it may also hurt or alienate the other person. When suspending judgment and allowing the other person, group or nation to find their own path and their own truth, we show compassion. We let go of misery and stress for ourselves, too. Wanting to be right raises our blood pressure and affects our stomach, heart and mind. Wanting to be right comes from a heart that is closed and a perspective that is too narrow.

Family

Holding my son in my arms, just after he had been born, was probably the most emotional and sacred moment in my life. I was the first person to greet him on his arrival, and looking into his soulful eyes reminded me of where I came from and what a precious responsibility it is to create and have a family. Family can provide the deepest love we have, although our children test our patience, push our limits and know where and how to push our buttons.

Expressing love in and for our family is the easiest and most difficult thing to do. Easy, as they are part of us and loving our children will normally come as second nature. Blood is thicker than water, as it is said, and most parents feel that. With most of us, we will always love our children no matter what, and they expect and deserve that without question. On the other hand, we want our children to do well and so we push, correct and try to influence and form them, all according to the beliefs we hold. Letting go of them and our influence over them can be difficult. Loving them and accepting them just as they are can be especially difficult. Our children mirror us, and we might struggle, perhaps, when we see our own weaknesses reflected in their personality. They might take after us or be very different; they might conform or rebel, always testing our patience, so we can often struggle. We want the best for them, but do we know what is best? Sometimes, in particular situations, we need to let go of that certainty.

For most of us, loving our children comes easily, and probably more so when they are babies, toddlers and young children, when we can guide and influence them gently. It becomes more difficult when they are rebellious teenagers, though; when they choose a profession that we do not think will suit them, or when they bring home a boyfriend or girlfriend we do not like. There may be times when they do not want to engage with life, or when they take drugs, wanting to escape. When they do not want to take responsibility, or think that what their parents say, do and think is old-fashioned. Despite and because of this, our family – our children, parents and siblings – provide the best opportunity for love. They are close to us – in our face – and we might not like that. They criticize us openly; they do not pay attention to what we say; they cheat on and lie to us, and still they are family. We expect to love them, but often we have to dig deep to do so. We might have to find our love for them again after they have hurt us. Family is our best testing ground for love, whether when we are part of a family as a child or whether we have created a family with a partner or spouse. It is within a family that we can find, give and receive true love.

Love – An Energy

Love is energy. We are energy. Energy needs to flow in order to be felt. In giving someone money, we might reward them. In expressing our love for them, we acknowledge them. We confirm who and what they are – love. Often we think that the other person knows we love them, so we do not have to say it. This might apply to our children, parents or friends. By not telling them, though, we just assume and rely on them knowing about our love for them. We need to tell them often, and in doing so we confirm to ourselves and to them who we both are – love; the energy of love.

Have you ever seen the face of your friend, brother or mother light up when you told them you loved them? Recently, I talked to my sister. She is very much a down-to-earth, no-nonsense person who would never think about spirituality or any of the subjects I often think about myself – I know, because she has told me so. Nevertheless, she looked after her mother-in-law, whom I too have known for decades, and who has since died of breast cancer. My sister would never make a fuss about it, or even mention it, had I not asked about it. But she is there, looking after people, as she did with her mother-in-law. Both my sister and I grew up with parents who were not able to express their love easily. As far back as I can remember, they never told us that they loved us. My sister is not used to being told by someone that they love her. I told her, and I felt my love, respect and gratitude for her at that very moment. She seemed embarrassed at first, but then her face lit up, and she was so very pleased. I had to tell her how much I love and admire her, as she is a true inspiration to me in her service to people. At the same time, I confirmed her as who and what she is – love; the energy of love.

Have you told your dearest today that you love them? If not, please do so, as we spread the energy of love that way. Sometimes, of course, doing so might be embarrassing, inconvenient or not appropriate, but prepare to be surprised, for that might not be the case after all! What we cannot do verbally, we can do in our hearts and minds. We can always bless the other person; connecting with our heart; smiling at them and maybe touching them gently, and in this way we send our love. What we cannot say in words can be said with a smile, with our gestures and posture, and with our heart open to them.

How can we change our world away from a perspective of fear in its many forms to one of love, if we do not confirm that we *are* love? Love is an energy that needs to spread; to be confirmed, strengthened, multiplied and freely given, and in telling others that we love them we do all this. We might just disregard who or what we truly are, until others tell us that they love us. In doing so we truly remind ourselves why we have come here – to spread love to all corners of the world. Being told we are loved, we will feel more confident that we can express love to others. We are love in process; we are the energy of love, so let us extend this love wherever possible. A word, however, does so much more than a gesture, so let us say "I love you" as often as we can.

Love and Hate

Love and hate are siblings. When we hate a person, we are saying that s/he is important enough for us to hate them. Hate has other, more distant relations too, like cousins: powerful resentment, dislike or strong reservations about someone; mistrust or a deep shadow in our heart about someone close to us. I read about people in Northern Ireland who were brought up by their parents to hate people of the other religion, and how difficult it was to let go of their hate. Many of them seem to have been, and are, aware of their hate, and how they came to have such strong feelings. At the same time, they had and have to work hard to overcome these feelings and turn them into love. That can only happen in stages and over time, in a process of letting go, forgiveness and healing of heart and mind.

In such a process – one of letting go – any of us might first come to a state of tolerance in which we learn to put up with the other person. This is a process that needs time and constant vigilance. Tolerance is a first step, but far from acceptance. With acceptance we allow others to be, though we might still dislike them. When exercising tolerance while communicating with those we used to hate, we start to see them as indoctrinated human beings, able to tell their own, often gruesome, story, and we can come to a point of greater acceptance. Despite lingering reservations, even dislike, we can reach a point of acceptance – not with our mind, but by truly opening our heart and actively burning off old feelings of hate and anger over time. In this process we are truly and slowly reborn; we shed the person we were and we change. In doing so, over time we make our world a safer place.

The path from hate to love can be a long journey that may take us years or decades. We might hate someone because we feel hard done to by them, and we struggle to forgive them for what they did. Tolerating and accepting them are first steps. Forgiving them and ourselves is the next, and the most important one. Forgiving ourselves is a process of remorse. With a willing and open heart we do not want to be that hating and angry person any more – the person who used to hate, the person who used to think about punishment and vengeance, the person with anger, resentment and misgivings in their heart. We do not just forgive ourselves (and having done so, become able to forgive others too), but we go through a deep process of remorse. In this process our fears – resentment, hate, intolerance, anger – peter out over time, our heart is being purified of them; we access, accept and drop these feelings over time. Through our courage and willingness to become a different person by actively letting go and living through forgiveness, we become a new person. Through a process that can be intense and long drawn out, we are reborn.

In the process of forgiving we start to develop love for the other person. In this, dislike and love are relatives – we can love, yet still dislike our relatives, or like them, but have not yet found a deep love for them. I have often started to like a person, too, once I had worked on forgiveness for myself while developing patience and finding inner peace. In this, compassion also overcomes dislike for ourselves, as well as concerning our struggle with the other person, what they have done and who they are. Are we not actors in the same play of life? After all, events and people are but opportunities to expand and learn; to shed our old self and become a better, more soul-motivated person. In the journey from hate to love we go from tolerance to acceptance; to forgiveness while disliking; to compassion and liking and loving, all the while unearthing unconditional love. It was only hidden, and finally we see the other person from a perspective of love again, instead of fear.

We start to love those who have done us wrong and those we hated by working with forgiveness – the energy of unconditional love and compassion. In our process of forgiveness we see the other person as a victim and creator, as someone who is a buddy in the game of life. They struggle, too, and as we are not perfect, neither are they. With compassion, and in connecting with humanitarian ideals, we allow our resistance to the notion of their being right to melt, along with our outrage at the injustice felt and the feeling that we were wronged. In working with forgiveness, over time hate can melt away. We begin to love the other person, knowing that all will pass in life, and over time we start to like and love them.

Our journey from hate to love might take many years. It may concern warring siblings; old spouses and former friends from childhood; people of other races or colours of skin; people of a different and 'wrong' faith, but we can all melt hate into love, although not usually overnight. Some might be blessed in experiencing a swift transformation of their hate into love. Most of us, though, have to and will work with a process that can take us years, a lifetime, or even generations (as in family feuds). Forgiveness is the key, and we are all in the same boat. It is truly possible, so please join me in the process of changing hate into love.

Sending Love Out into the World!

Driving to work the other day, I was listening to a love song – there are so many of them. While I was moved emotionally, as one sometimes is, I wondered why so many songs speak of love, and mostly romantic love. Having been alerted to this, I listened to many songs in the ensuing days, only to find that most of them, in some form other, dealt with the same topic.

For a moment I was tempted to think that this is an expression of the strength of love in our world. But I doubted this, and for a few days I spent time watching younger and older couples who looked as if they could be in love. I watched many young couples, some of whom who looked to be in love, but more of whom seemed to have fallen out of love. I watched couples sitting opposite or next to each other; walking together or doing their shopping, and it seemed to me that for them, love might have been lost. What seemed to be missing was a spark, a certain energy between them. Smiles and gentle gestures, an emotional and postural indication of wanting to care and protect each other, a subtle touch, a reassuring nod or smile, a tenderness that goes along with love.

I felt that the high occurrence of the love theme in songs was a sign of the absence of love within so many of us. We are probably touched by a song, and buy and listen to it, as we want and need a reminder to bring love into this world. Just as we all want to see the love so aptly described in the songs to be present in our world, we also need to express and spread love in this world. What our world needs is not just love in a romantic sense, as with courting couples, but love in its many forms. Love between parents and children, siblings and friends, colleagues (yes, colleagues), between teammates, among children, and especially between man and man; not just the "You okay buddy?" kind of greeting, but love between all of us; love in its many forms. From the subtle to the overt, love needs to go out into our world.

Our world is starved of love, and I believe that our frequent references to, and our songs, thoughts and feelings about love, are an expression of lack; of the absence of love. If love were very much present, our world would not be steeped in war, conflict and competition. Our love would go out to others more (as it often does when disaster strikes and the severity of human misery touches our heart), and it would very much change our world. There is love in the world, of course, otherwise our world would be in a much worse shape. However, love is needed, daily and constantly, to make our world a much, much better place. At present we compete for resources and wealth; for jobs and security; we fail to share enough of what we have and we defend our way of life. Too many of us feel righteous, and believe that our model of the world is the one to follow.

While some of us are blessed to be able to express love on a wider and more visible scale, and might be in the news, having devoted our lives to serving (as Mother Teresa was and others still are), most of us serve within the small daily world we live in. Love is expressed as simply as helping a neighbour; allowing someone to go first in a queue; working with the intensive process of forgiveness; a reassurance through a smile or a few words – there is an abundance of gestures which can express love.

A while ago, I was working on a project and learning about some software. The woman teaching us smiled frequently, and admitted it would take time to learn the system. Reassuringly, she often touched the students on their arm or shoulder, smiling gently. I saw these smiles and touches as small and yet big gestures of love that said "Be gentle with yourself – there is no rush and you will get there." I felt reassured, and I am sure that just as I remember her fondly, so will others in the group. No special occasion is necessary to bring love into our world, to express and extend love. Each of our lives constantly offers situations to remember who we are as love, and to extend ourselves as such. Often we seem to be oblivious as to what is an expression of love. Each little gesture, each smile, each forgiving and accepting, each feeling of sympathy towards another person and oneself – all these and more are expressions of love.

We are love, and we are called to perpetuate the energy that we are. Let us spread love into our world so that with time, when listening to love songs we become certain they are a truer expression of the world we live in. Join me in making ours a world in which love is in abundant supply.

Body and Soul

Some time ago, I was walking past what seemed to be a home for retired people. A woman in front was walking with a Zimmer frame. I wanted to get a glimpse of her, and having caught up with her, I saw the most beautiful wrinkled face looking at me. Her lovely blue eyes were radiant, and she gave me a kind smile. I stopped to talk with her, and during our short conversation I felt her soul shining through. What an impact she has had, as I can still remember her vividly. Why is that? As I said, I felt her soul shining through strongly, and knew she was near the end of her time on Earth. I saw beauty in an old and very tired body, too, and felt grateful for the reminder of how we live through a lifelong journey.

Our western world seems to be obsessed with the body. Attempting to hide the ravages of age, we advertise the advantages of physical attributes in different ways. Some take to cosmetic surgery, others enhance their looks with clothes, makeup or bodybuilding. I recall a time as a 16-year-old when I thought I was not tall enough, complaining to my father about my lack of height. To this very day I remember my pleasure when I grew to just over 6 feet 2 inches during the next few years, having been a late developer. Some of my former girlfriends were self-conscious about their lack of bust, their thinness of hair or other issues, and I suppose most of us can find reasons to complain about our physical appearance.

Loving ourselves includes loving our physical bodies too. We might not like our personality, but with time and perseverance we are able to change it. We become more patient, for example, as we work on our listening skills, or we become more compassionate and kind as we let go of selfish tendencies. It is indeed possible to change our personality. Beyond the few measures mentioned above, it is more difficult to change our physical appearance. Therefore we do well in accepting the looks we were born with and have developed into our adulthood. Moreover, we know that as much as we might want to ignore our changing body over time, wrinkles will appear. We might find it more difficult to melt away the fat around our midriff, and our muscles become less lean and are more difficult to build up. When we do physical work or sport at a later age, we need more time to recover, and suffer more strongly afterwards. Our eyesight weakens too, whether as a result of computer use or because of the passage of time.

Loving ourselves includes loving and caring for our bodies, as they are the vehicles through which we experience the world. Our body and soul are closely connected. Often our soul gives us a push or reminder, we receive messages from our body about feeling ill at ease, or when dis-ease presents itself. We can love and nourish our body with healthy food, exercise and rest, and by letting go of our fearful need to numb our experience of the world with mind-altering substances such as alcohol. Loving our body from and with soul; listening to our higher guidance from soul, we can relinquish our role in wanting to avoid aging. We start to see what our youth obsession truly is: a fear of rejection and loneliness as we lose our attractiveness. Realizing this, we are asked to shower ourselves with compassion and kindness. Living from soul, we learn to perceive, embrace and rejoice in the wonderful beauty in the aging face of the wise woman – the 'crone', and the wise man – the 'sage'.

Our body carries us for a lifetime: through the world, through all of our experiences, and through all of our thoughts and emotions, seeking always to do its very best to protect and support us even in those times when we might be doing our very best to self-destruct. Our body is a subtle, finely-tuned barometer that shows us the degree of health we possess, depending on how we choose to live in this world. It is through our body that we experience the joy of vitality when we are living in a harmonious and loving way, and it is our body that tells us, through the physical manifestations of dis-ease, when we are living in an imbalanced and fearful way. In loving body and soul, we arrive at this understanding at some point, and we will find peace within the harmony of body and soul – in times of health and illness, too.

Loving the Now

How often do we feel sandwiched between the past and the future? Sometimes we listen to a golden oldie or watch an old film and it takes us back to our past, to our youth. Watching the film, we are reminded how much fun we had then and how little responsibility, and we might yearn to go back to those carefree times. Reminiscing, we might also become aware of how time has changed us – we see wrinkles, a memory that has started to show some gaps, and a body that is not as smooth and slim as it used to be. With too many memories of challenging times, we have buried the joy and fun we used to feel.

By denying feelings of grief and loss we only give them additional strength. What we repress returns to us more strongly. It serves us better to recognize these feelings and let them be. Grief and sadness come and go – they are signs of a life well lived. At the same time, we can let go too: there is no need to wallow in our feelings. The now is always here to be enjoyed; to be seen, felt and experienced. Within the last decade our future seems to have become more uncertain. We might worry about our finances and job security, about finding a suitable partner or simply being sure we are making the right decisions. Our media bombard us with mostly negative news. We may be concerned about our environment, feel uncertain about our government, worry about the education of our children or whether we will be looked after in our old age.

Thinking and mourning about the past, as well as worrying about the future, keeps us in a constant state of anxiety. Only in the now do we find comfort and peace, as it takes away from past and future concerns. I have developed a love affair with the present, while being aware of the past and future. Like most of us, I reminisce about the past on the odd occasion, and take steps towards a better future. However, it is this present moment that provides, and by breathing deeply and just being here I feel tremendous comfort. As a spirit and soul on a human journey, we face challenges indeed. However, when we focus on this very moment, we can feel peace. This moment does not have any concerns – our pain from the past is just a memory, and our future concerns never arrive. We live in the permanent flow of life, and when we focus on this flow, past and future are just what has been and what might be.

This moment provides ample opportunity to see, watch and feel the joy and peace that are our birthrights. We may look at a sunset or observe a toddler taking her first steps; becoming aware of the need to breathe deeply from our belly, connecting with our heart centre, and in doing so, also connecting with a deeper and more peaceful aspect of who we are. When listening to someone in need and truly empathizing with him, we are comforted to know that we are all in the same boat. Smiling at a stranger and getting a smile back; blessing the other driver who took our right of way and wishing him a safe journey; feeling into our body and noticing we are relaxed, healthy and alert; listening to birds singing outside; listening to ourselves, to a deeper and wiser part of soul and feeling comforted; asking your guardian angel to let herself be known and felt to you, thus feeling spiritual comfort and security; or thinking about someone we love and feeling that love in our heart. In this moment we have the opportunity to reassure ourselves about our priorities. We acknowledge that despite past grief and future concerns we have arrived here safely. Connect with the here and now, and experience how without fail it gives you comfort. In this moment we just *are*, while not ignoring past or future.

We can and do focus on a positive outcome in our future. We work towards success, focusing our thoughts and hearts on it. We hope, and might pray, as this provides comfort. Revisiting our past, we notice how bitter and resentful we might feel towards a person or situation; about a loss or a 'failure'. As we possess memory, we cannot ever escape our past, but our past is just memory, and it is only when we reconnect with our memory that we evoke bitterness, regret or anger. Here again it is the now that provides comfort. Breathing deeply and relaxing, we can acknowledge the feelings that have been brought up by our memory, and at the same time let them go. We are safe now, and while we are not ignoring the past, in this moment we are safe. The past reaches us via memory only, and by breathing and relaxing and calming our busy, reminiscing mind, we are safe right here.

The past reaches us indeed, albeit via memory and resulting feelings, but we remember and revisit it through memory only. We cannot completely escape from wanting to create a safe and secure future either, but this moment provides all the comfort we need. We can develop a love story with our now. Ask yourself, your higher self, your guardian angel or a friend to remind you to connect with now at this moment. Write it on a wall or sticker – our relationship with now is beautiful. You find peace in this, and it spills over into the past and future too. Over and over again, do it – it does work.

Where Does Love Take Us?

Do we ever know where love will take us? Love might simmer away at low temperature or boil over in a way that completely consumes us. For some of us this happens in a personal relationship; less frequently in our love for family, our nation or mankind. We think, for example, that passion belongs to the young. However, as an older friend in her sixties told me, she has recently been totally consumed with passion in a relationship with an older man, and she had never thought that would be possible. How could passion consume her this way in her sixties? She felt this passion in her soul and heart, but it included a strong sexual energy too.

A fulfilling expression of love through sexual pleasure requires our alertness, our honesty and courage, for it is a delightful and intriguing game, a graceful dance and a clever and subtle exchange of energy. We will never make love with two different people, or with the same person on two occasions, in quite the same way. Sex is also a river in which no man can step into the same place twice. It requires us to be aware in every moment, and to act from and with our unconditionally loving soul. Physical love is not easy – the manner of pleasure and sexuality are unique to each person. There is no universal recipe, but that is what makes physical love so exciting. When we are young we might be impatient and unable to control the awakening force of physical love within ourselves. When we are old, our body might need more time and patience: the force of youth has gone, but now there is inner peace, joy and greater expertise. When we make love unconditionally from soul, it creates a connection with our partner that deeply intensifies our expression and experience of love. We are, each of us, love, and when we join together in the act of physical love, we become a wonderful, joyous expression of love in motion.

But love will take us in other directions, too – it is not just restricted to physical energy. I was on the phone with my sister today while she was working in her garden. Talking to her, and knowing how hard she works, I felt an immense wave of love welling up within. I expressed this in my concern for her physical wellbeing, asking her to slow down, take more rests and smell the roses. I knew she felt my expression of love in my words of care and concern. Whilst growing up in a German miner's family it was never easy to express love openly as we did not experience that as children, she understood and appreciated my sudden outburst of care and love.

An expression of love can move mountains and grabs our attention enormously. At a moment like this, we might struggle to contain the love rising from within, as it wants to burst out and be expressed. But the energy of love needs to become contagious by flowing out into the world: from brother to sister, husband to wife, parent to child and vice versa; between friends and colleagues; groups; nations – in short, all over the world. While we might struggle to express it as it can feel overwhelming, let us have the courage to unleash it anyway. As embarrassing as it might feel and look, we will feel the better for it, and so will the receiving person or group. Love contained is love hidden; love not expressed is a missed opportunity to make this world a better place.

Love cannot and does not want to be controlled. It wants to take any form that heals our wounds and soothes our minds and hearts. Love is like an Olympic torch: it needs to move from person to person, nation to nation, and in all forms possible. It expresses itself by accepting our differences, through compassion for those struggling with life and facing their own demons, via a quiet care for a sister, brother or relative, or by developing the patience within that allows another to learn their own lessons, even when we feel tempted to step in and explain.

Love can express itself as a deep affinity for nature, trees, rivers and animals; like poets we can feel inspired by walking in nature. We might fall in love with someone who is just not our type. Very recently, someone told me she had fallen in love with a labourer – a rough man, not very educated; someone who likes his drink, rugby and football, while she is highly educated and into art, poetry and the opera. We never know where love might take us, or how love can and will shape our being. The energy of soul and love finds its expression in many forms, as long as we allow it to. Let us all be open to being consumed by love. Recognizing that we are that very expression of love, we can be willing to let love take us where we need to go and become what we must.

Love Yourself – Love Others

A few years ago I met a woman who was a devoted mum, and who very much cared for and loved her children. Life had not treated her well in some respects, but she was surely dedicated to her family, as well as to a great circle of friends. She loved to be of service in many ways. As friends, we discussed the issue of love. I casually asked her whether she loved herself, and she blushed. "No," she said. "How can I be so selfish as to love myself? My life is all about loving others." I did not know how to respond to that at the time, so I just smiled and did not say anything.

Thinking about it recently, though, I remembered other people like her, and that I have heard this kind of statement a good few times before. Are we really selfish if we love ourselves? Especially, as I have been asked before, when wanting to love unconditionally – is it not that we only love unconditionally if we love others more than ourselves? Loving ourselves seems to be regarded as a sort of indulgence by some. But how can we truly love others if we cannot and do not love ourselves? In that very decision we have declared our love conditional.

When we love ourselves, including those bits of our personality we are not entirely happy with, we can do so for others. When we love our shortcomings, we can accept those in others. Knowing that we can improve our personality and beliefs, we accept others can too. Without loving ourselves, as we judge ourselves, we might also be judgmental and not accepting of others, with their impatience, intolerance, anger and prejudices. Knowing this, we have the opportunity to look more deeply into what we do not like about others. Whatever we struggle to accept and embrace within them is very likely what we dislike within ourselves, too. On the other hand, when we love ourselves in a lifelong process, warts and all, we can offer this to others.

I have also met people who seem to 'love' themselves too much – *if we can call this love* – and such people seem to be the centre of their own universe. Often they proclaim that they have no regard for others. As a former colleague once said "All is well with me. I had a tough life too, so why should I care for others? I only have enough capacity to care for myself." We might indeed think we do not have the capacity to love others, except perhaps close family, as our wounds are too deep for us to be capable of loving or caring for others. Feeling cheated by life, we might feel that we can get our own back by not caring for anyone else. Maybe we were never encouraged to care for others as a child.

Some of us will have had a very tough childhood in which care, love and emotional intimacy were in short supply. Our parents were not able to extend love to us – prestige, career and status always came first, and we were starved of love-nutrition. In this situation, though, we have the choice to perpetuate or change it within our own life; with our children, friends and beyond. Being overly focused on ourselves makes for a lonely life. Prestige, power, money and influence can provide superficial satisfaction, as we seem to get from life what we put into it. However, life always mirrors our inner qualities. When we do not love and care for ourselves and others – not just with security, but by truly accepting and loving who we are – those with loving qualities are not very likely to enter our life. Or we might not even notice if and when they are present, as our focus is elsewhere.

I trust that for each of us there can come a time, even if in our dying moments only, when we realize how selfish, self-centred and thus lonely our life has been. But life provides clues all the time – situations or people, reminders and alerts – and we can pay attention to our loving soul-self; our expression of soul, compassion and kindness, again and again, and change our ways at any time. What is the right amount of love for self and others? We decide for ourselves, do we not? When being too self-centred, we might miss the opportunity to be of service. We fail to feel fulfilled, and lack true purpose in life. By not loving ourselves, warts and all, our love for others will be limited. What we have not embraced within, we struggle to accept without. Life is about balancing self-centredness with selflessness.

Love – No Matter What

Some time ago, I was on a dating website and told a friend about it. We discussed love in a romantic relationship, dating, expectations and experiences. She laughed, as she felt that there is a simple recipe for lasting love. She has for a long time been married to a man who is about 20 years older than her. They are both teachers and have two children. "Claus," she said, "when you have found the right person, you do not ever question your relationship. You just love them no matter what." This comment surprised me and has been on my mind ever since. Loving 'no matter what' suggests that once we have found a partner, we make our relationship happen as long as we love 'no matter what'. There seems to be evidence for that, especially in couples from an older generation. I have had the privilege to know couples who have succeeded that way and have had lifelong and happy relationships.

'No matter what' speaks of acceptance and deep commitment; about 'true love', and, I would guess, needs honest and true communication. We need to love from the core of who we are; from soul. Loving someone 'no matter what' helps us to resist temptation when someone else enters our life, and it indicates that we can learn to love someone 'no matter what' even though this person might not be the most suitable for us. Moreover, our partner might change considerably from the person we used to know. Love can conquer problems and challenges. 'No matter what' indicates that we can continue to love someone over a long period of time, especially if the relationship is based on friendship, too. 'No matter what' – certainly inspiring and motivating, and a soothing concept and attitude.

On the other hand, we might rob ourselves of the opportunity to grow and develop in a different direction, as perhaps we could expand more with a different person. Looking at our society, long-term relationships seem to have become a thing of the past. Overall, some might think that a soulmate or knight in shining armour will come into their life, whereas others see life as a series of opportunities for learning and expansion with a number of partners. Do we not learn and expand in and through relationships? If so, we might want to seek a new partner, if mutual growth no longer seems possible.

However, our strong emotional ties might make that difficult, as we have feelings of possessiveness or strong commitments, and struggle to let go and move on. Many a breakup seems to be messy and painful. Our partner might see love-commitment as a lifelong story and struggle to let go of us in friendship. At times we might want to end a relationship because we see a different future: one person wants to buy a property and settle down as s/he wants a family, for example, while the other is focused on a career or travelling, not wanting to 'sacrifice' their way of life for a family. While neither is right or wrong, it can and often does lead to a breakup.

We might think there is one special soulmate out there and want to love 'no matter what', or see life as a series of opportunity for growth and expansion by using and developing all our faculties with different partners. Of course, there is nothing to say that we cannot achieve that with one special person.

During my life, I had a long relationship with a woman who was very intellectual and intelligent, at a time when I was going to university as a mature student, while later I was married to a woman who was pursuing a spiritual path at a time when this issue had also started to become important to me. Is there a correct answer? Probably not. Maybe we need to be with different partners until we find the one we can stay with for the rest of our life. I certainly hope so. Or we move from one partner to the next, sometimes elegantly and easily; sometimes causing heartbreak and needing forgiveness. At times it might be best for us to be on our own for a while, too. Life offers choice, does it not? 'No matter what' offers an enticing prospect indeed! Those of us who are able to live with a partner for a long time and feel cherished, while simultaneously being able to continue to grow and expand with that partner 'no matter what' are truly blessed.

Love and Death

Love and Death seem a strange combination to write about. But it is death that sharpens our heart towards expressing love. Death defines life and love. In the knowledge we will die one day, we are reminded to live each day from a heart filled with love. If not today, when? One day we will live the last part of our story in a human body, letting go and cutting our ties, and it will be too late then to live from soul and love. Our limited life span can and does serve as a constant reminder to express the energy of the love we are to the utmost of our ability.

Some people die with the regret of not having loved enough, of not having stayed in sufficient contact with friends and family. It is too late then – we can never turn back the clock. Some might believe that we live many lives, so there will be other opportunities to express different aspects of ourselves as divine love. Others adopt a more existentialist approach and believe this is the only life we live. In any case, death sharpens our awareness of the fact that time is limited; our time to express the love we are in a human body is limited. We might believe that we are timeless and continue to live as a spirit, but nonetheless this is the life that offers us the greatest opportunity to experience and express love. We are asked to express love to the fullest of our ability. In our choice between fear and love; hate and love, we are encouraged to consciously choose love each day.

Death serves as a daily reminder to focus on love. Ask for the grace to express who you are through friendship, acceptance, kindness and compassion, and the expressing of the love you are in its many forms.

Some of us have lost people close to us early in life. Often those relatives or friends who left early expressed their love to us very strongly while they were alive. It is as if they knew of their limited life span, and it reminded them to express love strongly. Impending death can do that. Whether we know that we are ill or we live from a perspective of living fully and consciously each day, or whether we know and feel that unconsciously, death sharpens our urge to be and our urge to embrace and express love.

This is not morbid. We can simply be aware of our limited time and because of that, be happy and aware. Knowing our time on Earth is finite, we are able to remind ourselves to live and engage with life more fully, to learn, grow and expand more fully, and above all, to love more fully. Death is a timely reminder. Many older people, being in their last phase of life, express more gratitude. Some, having been angry and disappointed in their earlier life, mellow with age. It seems as if they feel reminded to make peace and connect with a deeper aspect within themselves. My dear father, for example, has become much kinder and more compassionate in his late seventies.

Death is a timely reminder to live and love to the fullest of our abilities. Buddhists strive to live with the awareness of limitation and death. They encourage us to die a little death each day. We are reminded to let go of all our attachments in many ways – our need for strong material comfort; our expectations and assumptions; our knowing and security – and to do so happily while embracing uncertainty. We can all let go of our right to be right; to hate and dislike; to moan and be grumpy; to see ourselves as victims who are tossed around by the uncertainties and insecurities of life. We let go and just be who we are. Death is a timely reminder that we are love! We can and want to discover, embrace and express who we are. Let us do this now together, letting death remind us daily of who we truly are beyond this body – spirit and soul; a divine being. We are love, and we are asked to use our limited time on Earth to express and extend who we are.

Love on the Rocks

Love on the Rocks, a famous song by Neil Diamond, tells of a situation most of us know about. Someone recently told me how devastated she was when her last romantic relationship ended, and that it took her two years to work through the emotional debris so she could be open to meeting someone special again. Interestingly, it was her who finished the relationship, as she felt that her partner was unable to make the commitment she was yearning for. No matter who finishes a relationship and how it happens, in most cases we face a period of emotional turmoil. A friend of mine, who had been in a relationship with a lovely woman for several years, fell in love with another woman, and overwhelmed by the depths of his emotions for this woman, finished the relationship with his girlfriend. Both of them are loving people, experienced in life, and neither had felt possessive of the other person or expected to be together for the rest of their lives.

But love was on the rocks for both of them. She had to face losing a relationship in which she had invested all of her emotions and love; he struggled to understand how and why he could have fallen in love with someone else, although he had loved his partner deeply. This dilemma brought up old patterns that drove him to the brink of insanity. It was with the help of therapy, healing and taking time off work that he was able to get through this intense period of change. His new romantic partner felt the strain of it all, too. I am pleased to say, though, that not only did they all survive, but the situation helped everyone involved to access deeper levels of love, acceptance and kindness within themselves, for one another and other people, too.

In a world of constant choice and change, we might develop expectations for our romantic relationships that can be unrealistic. Often we feel we want to hold onto him/her, as they are viewed as a rock in a world of turmoil. Our partner is seen as a constant in a world that changes and forces us to go along with change. When our partner threatens to go away, or changes in a way we do not like, we can feel threatened and lost. A friend of mine who divorced her husband of a few years told me that what had most disturbed him was the way she had changed. When going to Relate, a counselling service for couples, he repeatedly said that he could not cope as she had changed so much. He just wanted his old wife back, the woman he fell in love with a few years ago.

While, so he thought, she had changed enormously, he felt he had stayed the same person. How can we stay the same person in an ever-changing world? Whereas her outlook on life had changed considerably, he, by his reckoning, had remained the same. However, while some of us seem to stay the same on the surface, our changes are more subtle and slow, and sometimes we might not be aware of them at all. 'Love on the rocks', as I have often seen, comes about as one person changes more than the other; because one wants a commitment the other person cannot give (marriage, moving in together or having children etc.); because one or both feels a strong desire to shift and change, perhaps to escape boredom; or maybe because the grass appears greener with someone else.

'Love on the rocks' forces us to deal with emotions we might not have felt for a long time: anger, grief and frustration. Working through these emotions takes time. We might feel cheated and betrayed; unloved and left behind, and working with these thoughts and feelings brings about a period of healing and change for everyone involved. The outcome is uncertain, though. Some of us might feel betrayed for the rest of our life, or, unable to forgive, perhaps harbouring a grudge against the other person for a long time. This shadow can darken any new relationship, too. But despite all the turmoil, most of us will come to a time of shifting and changing. While we might not be able to forgive and continue to harbour ill feelings, there will come a time when we will let go to some extent and move on. Most of us learn and change through our grief. We gain positive insights, even if only in hindsight. 'Love on the rocks' can and does lead to growth and maybe forgiveness, and we are able to love again.

Love and Loss

Someone I had known for 40 years died very recently, while another very close friend was very suddenly taken to hospital and is now in intensive care. My sister underwent an operation for the treatment of cancer and the prognosis for complete healing is uncertain, while a former colleague told me that she underwent an operation recently. What a reminder of potential and actual loss! Many of us have faced loss, and those who left us behind will always have a place in our heart. The fates of others tell us that love and loss, like love and death, are twin sisters.

Sometimes it takes an incident, like sudden illness, to remind us that we might have taken someone for granted. They may well have been in our thoughts and hearts, but have we truly connected with them recently? Do we check on them, send them healing thoughts, meet them for a coffee, smile and laugh with them? The prospect of loss brings home the precariousness of life. It is now that we are asked to express and share our love with those close to us. It will be too late when they are gone.

Having faced loss myself, those close to me are always in my heart and thoughts. My mum, my favourite aunts, my grandfather and grandmother, close friends I lost and a love that was taken from me. That will never change. They are present to me often – in my contemplation and meditation. Many of those who have crossed my path, different people at different times and whether they are now dead or alive, are often present to me. As our time on Earth is limited, we can all remind ourselves how those close to us need our attention: meeting them for a coffee, a short and loving email, a spontaneous phone call. We see an article of interest and send it to them; we catch up after weeks, months or even years with little or no contact, and in doing so we convey a simple message: "I love you, I care for you, and although I might not always be in touch, I still think of you and you will always have a place in my heart."

The story of life is common to all of us, albeit with different characters and plots, and leading to different insights and experiences. But we all share a world, and as beings of love, we can share our love. We do so by taming prejudices and reservations towards those far away and those who are different to us. We endeavour to accept – not just tolerate – those who have a different background or beliefs, and we can certainly care and express our love more actively for those closest to us.

While a sudden illness or the prospect of death can be a timely reminder to tell and show those closest to us how much we do love them, we can always take love-action without a reminder. It takes a few minutes here and there to send an email or a text; an hour to meet for a coffee. We can send some uplifting lines, just to stay in touch with those closest to us. They are our true opportunity to express who we are – love in action. Please do contact them now; extend the love you are to those closest to you – NOW.

The Greatest Healer

Love, and we as the extensions of love, are the greatest healer in our fearful world. Recently I have seen enormous healing between people, both on a personal and a wider level. Through a process of reconciliation in South Africa, for example, healing took place between those who have committed atrocities and those who experienced those atrocities, mostly through a process of voicing the pain by those on the receiving end – and being listened to.

A friend of mine had been living through a period of deep pain. His wife had cheated on him, and when he found out he finished their relationship very quickly. She had taken advantage of him financially, emptying their bank account before their separation and divorce, and had moved to a location unknown to him. His first reaction was an urge to track her down and take revenge. But he allowed himself to take some time before reacting, and chose to focus on himself for healing instead. Apart from going to work, he did not leave his flat for two years. He saw his wife's behaviour as an incentive to dig deep and face his own demons; to have a very close look at himself and work with forgiveness. Over time he came to a point of forgiveness for himself, and for her, too. A few years later, synchronistically, she came back into his life, just when he had forgiven himself and everyone involved.

Today they enjoy a friendship again. Both see the divorce and the ensuing pain as a huge opportunity to forgive. Both feel they have learned and found acceptance, and have grown as human beings. Forgiveness and acceptance are both expressions of love. Forgiving ourselves and others is love in process; love in action. This kind of love heals our wounds. Love is the greatest healer. When we go to a therapist or through a period of soul-searching, whether as a nation, a family or as an individual, we connect with the deepest aspect of who we are. Any method of therapy or healing is a form of love. Without accessing the love we are – the divine expression of love – there will be no healing.

Sometimes we undergo a period of therapy, but healing and change will not come to us. Maybe we are still reacting from a perspective of fear, churning through our challenging experiences in our mind, while our heart remains distant. While our heart is distant, we do not connect on the level of soul and divine love, and if we fail to see ourselves from a perspective of who we truly are – spirit and soul – we will not heal. We might try different methods and approaches; go from one therapy and therapist to the next, but we are not healing. Love is the greatest healer. When we truly acknowledge who we are: a spiritual being with a soul on a human journey; when we recognize, embrace and express who we are, we set in motion deep healing. We might not then need a therapist. Love is the strongest and only healer, and healing is always a change of perspective from fear to love.

When we create with fear in any of its many expressions, we create more fear and animosity. We might give in to our prejudices and intolerance; we want to be right; we may want to escape into soulless activities such as drug-taking, watching mindless entertainment, bingeing on food or alcohol, drama and gossip, all these being expressions of fear – and in doing so, we feed fear further. Fear is simply an absence of light, and fear keeps love masked. But love is stronger, as it embraces all of us. We express the love we are when we make the choice to let go of fear. In this process we might stumble; we struggle and slip, but over time we will find, embrace and express the love we are. Expressing the love we are we can heal ourselves, any difficult situation, and our past and future. Through living our love in the present we heal our family rifts and our prejudices, and fear among groups and nations. Love is the deepest healer. Let us connect with the depth we are and start our journey of healing today. Let us embrace the love we are and heal our world. Please join me in this.

Love and Courage

It takes courage to find understanding of love; to acknowledge, embrace and express the love we are. In our fearful world, relationships mirror the uncertainties, fears and insecurities of living, and expressing our love in a relationship takes courage. Extending all shades of love into our world – compassion, kindness and acceptance – takes guts, and even more so, I believe, for a man. I can still remember the strange looks I received from former colleagues when they wanted to know more about me and I told them that I worked with healing. Apparently, kindness and compassion were not desirable in a sales job that thrives on competition. All were facing an ever-upward target. Sales is about beating the competition, being tough and being a winner. A good salesperson has an attitude of achieving; of wanting to be the best in the team, and these attitudes were appreciated. What a great experience it was, though. Having to face targets and constant competition, I realized my preference to express love, not fear; kindness instead of competition; compassion, not judgment.

It needs courage to want to understand who we are with regards to love. It takes patience to explore the energy we are, and it takes heart-intelligence to truly understand the subtleties of love. When we explore and acknowledge the energy of the love we are, we set in motion a process of change that cannot be stopped. Release the genie and you will never go back to where you were before. This is the highest service we give to ourselves and our world – our courage to explore, embrace and so truly express the energy of love we are, especially in our fearful and competitive world. When expressing the love we are, we might be looked at with suspicious eyes. With a smile on our face, an open heart and a peaceful mind, we might be secretly admired, but also seen as a dreamer; someone who is not suited to this world. I remember how, as a child, I did not like this fearful world. I just wanted to be, to play and to express my joy of living. Going to school; having to sit still for hours and learn things which I felt would not truly serve me on a soul-level but only the world we live in, I cried for years. I did not want to go to school, and for years I felt ashamed as I cried in front of the teacher and fellow pupils. My poor mother did not know what to do with me, and I remember how she and my dad felt relieved when I finally accepted, toughened up and got on with the process of learning in school.

In exploring the love we are, we will encounter the shadows we have taken on board. We need utmost courage to see, accept and embrace these shadows, too. Working through our darker energies, we encounter parts of ourselves we do not like – jealousy, envy or a highly competitive mind – as I had developed through growing up in a very competitive German society. Letting these and others go, and thus shifting from fear to love, is a process; a journey that takes courage and commitment. While doing so we might look small and vulnerable; we might not function well and may feel out of sync with the world. We could view ourselves as a failure or an outcast, but if we want to truly become and express who we are – a divine being in human form – we need to work through our shadow energy. Letting go can take years of committed introspection. In the world to come, though, this process is quickening, and more of us will be able to embrace and express our true nature more rapidly.

Once our shadow energies have shifted, we are increasingly at ease to express who we are. Through our shadow work we start to shed light on who we are. When embracing and expressing who we truly are, we gain the confidence, peace, and yes, serenity, to just be and to live with joy. We find the courage within to show our true being to the world. Courage will find us, as we increasingly let go of worries and start to trust in our soul's path, perhaps trusting that the universe is looking after us all the time. Often, it is then that we find a partner with whom we can express our love. When we have become the energy of joy, we attract those we can grow and express with: as romantic lovers, business partners, or friends who help us, as we do them, in many ways. Fellow souls on a similar path find each other easily, as we are drawn to the energy of those who also express their divine love.

Love takes courage. The courage to truly want to understand the love we are; to acknowledge all aspects of ourselves, including our shadows; to embrace all; to let go of what is no longer needed and to express who we truly are. When we live our divine joy and express and extend the universal love we are, we might face resistance from many. But love tears down resistance. Living from and being of the energy of love, we provide an example to follow. We might influence in ways we cannot yet understand. All it takes is our intention. Let us all summon the heart-courage to fully express the love we are, no matter where we are now.

Is There a Particular Way?

The expressions of love are many, as are the manner of our rediscovery, our deeper understanding, our acknowledgment, our embracing and extension of love. Some of us go about it quietly, with a kind word to a neighbour, a helping hand to a colleague, a smile for a stranger or compassion and patience for those who struggle. They express who they are in subtle but effective ways. Some work as teachers, helping others to strengthen their understanding of who they are; reminding them and offering them tools to do so. Some of us work as therapists, helping others to discard their remaining shadows. Writers use words and the energy behind them to remind, teach and encourage us to be who we are. Entrepreneurs bring us jobs that allow us to feel safe financially and thus have the peace to explore the love we are as divinity. Our jobs offer the opportunity for us to be great colleagues at work – another place where we can express and extend the love we are.

Sometimes our love is disguised, and we have to be tough to be kind. Seeing someone on drugs, or those who have lost their loving expression, we can remind them with clear and honest – but also kind – words. In this we do not allow any excuse, thus reminding the other person that they can choose to drop their perception of being a victim. Sometimes we might have to finish a romantic relationship, knowing that both of us can grow further without the other, thus letting go of comfort and companionship. As a parent, the safety of our children is our concern and we need to caution and safeguard our young ones, albeit with kindness, although we would love them to be completely free in their movements.

Never is love as straightforward as we might think, and there is no one particular way of expressing. Love comes in shades of strength. Some are able to love close family only, vigorously defending them against others. They might feel that others – whether their own society or those of different cultures – could invade and hurt their family. This can change during a lifetime to include friends, colleagues, fellow believers from a church, or even a nation. Others start to see themselves as part of a soul-family that extends beyond family and friends; beyond culture, belief and colour of skin; beyond nations and towards a brotherhood of wo/men. In a vast cosmos comprising multiple dimensions and universes, we might come to an understanding of our potentially awesome expansion as divine beings, and we embrace all there is. In this, nothing is better or worse – there is no hierarchy of love, only different expressions. Ultimately we are all expressing the strongest, widest and deepest; the most encompassing energy of love we are at any given moment.

The more we drop our reservations; our shadows and prejudices; our intolerances and judgments, the more we peel off to reach a level of unconditional love where we are able to encompass all. That includes the animals and plants on our planet. The way we treat everything in nature – trees, rivers, oceans, our soil and animals – truly shows the level of love we have achieved. True and unconditional love includes animals, too – our soul brothers and sisters – as well as plants and rocks. The way we treat Mother Earth at present, one might think we were still barbarians. In our ignorance of understanding, in failing to see the Earth as a living and breathing, compassionate and very aware host for our bodies and souls, we treat her with utter disrespect.

In our journey towards deeper love, on our path to understanding, acknowledging, expressing and extending the love we are and have, we need to come to a point where we all include our benign and highly intelligent host. We need to embrace all there is over time, and in this process we come to a point of feeling safe and secure within. Arriving there, we can let go of competition, envy and jealousy. When we feel peace and serenity within, we are able to deepen and widen our love without.

There is no particular way of love, as all expressions are welcome, from the subtle and small to the big and grand. In time we can all develop the compassion of a Mother Teresa or the serenity of a Buddha. We will understand that all religions offer the same curriculum of love, even though the misinterpretation of some has also led to righteousness, bigotry and violence. In the meantime, let us all deepen our love, working with the energy of love we have and are. In time, though, we will, more and more, come to share a particular way of love. A way of unconditional and divine love that embraces all of mankind, nature, our planet and beyond. Let us start today, please.

◈ SUCCESS ◈

Success means different things to all of us. We might seek success through a business we are developing, or by climbing the employment ladder. Others look for recognition through social pursuits, or academic and intellectual achievements. Many of us want to be great parents and partners to our loved ones. We might want to be very successful in sports, or we may measure success through our social standing, in terms of prestige, influence or good looks. High social standing and influence might give us the feeling and 'certainty' of success. Yet others will see spiritual evolvement as success, developing divine qualities like compassion, kindness, inner peace and serenity, or maybe a deeper understanding of why we are here, how best to live and act, or how to shape our unfolding story in a loving, rather than fearful, way.

How do we know that we are successful? While this can seem obvious, as rich and successful people can display material possessions, appear in the media or live the life they want, recognizing success can also be more subtle. What kind of personal qualities would we need to be successful? How can success unfold, if at all? Can success have a deeper meaning and serve a purpose other than just the obvious? Success is a process; an attitude and a state of mind which needs belief, and for most of us does not come overnight. Success is a complex subject, and the following humble thoughts can only scratch the surface of a deeper issue.

You Are Alive

You have made it. You are alive. You have a story – certain parents; a particular country you live in. You are tall, short, bald or handsome; you have a pleasant or fiery personality. All this is part of the story you have been creating. When we look at success, we often have a certain expectation as to how it should look. You are success, whatever you do, because you are here and because you are participating in our common story. You touch people, you talk – even if you cannot talk – and you express yourself. You might be blind, or handicapped in any other way, but you are still expressing divinity with your body and your actions, just by being yourself. You cannot but participate. Even if you do not want to engage with life, you are doing so as others will see you as not wanting to engage with life. Having an attitude of not wanting to engage with life is engaging, even though we might not want to see it that way.

You cannot fail to be successful, as you are in this life. Simply being in life, whatever the form of expression, is success already. Worldly success in terms we often cherish – money, fame, prestige – are just another form that we adore. We can accept, run after and worship them, but make no mistake: you are success already. You came with the intention of participating, of making your mark (even if you refuse to do so), of making friends and influencing others, of being an example – whether in a loving or unpleasant way. You have done so already, and you continue to do so, therefore you are a resounding success.

Success – Not Always a Straight Line

When looking at successful people, we often see the end result of hard work and years of trials and tribulations. We do not see the process of success, though, so we only pay attention to the end result. We see a famous actress and forget how many years of training she had. We see a successful businessman, but do not realize that he failed twice before achieving success. We see a loving psychologist who is so influential and empathetic with her clients, but do not know how often she herself experienced depression. Having personally learnt how to overcome depression, she now uses her knowledge to help other people. We see a famous singer and tend to ignore the fact that he went to many auditions where he was turned down. Believing in his talent, he persevered, though, and slowly success came his way. If we knew of the challenges preceding success, we might never even start or take any action. It is our belief, our trust and perhaps a streak of stubbornness that help us on the way. When looking back years later, we cherish the hard work and we clearly see the process leading to success. It has never been a straight line, even though it might look that way to others.

Patience and Perseverance

Success has never come easily to me. We all hear stories about people who achieve success, seemingly overnight or in an easy fashion. But I believe the truth is that these examples, often sensationalized by our press, are an exception to the rule. Whether we want to succeed in our own business or university career, as a good parent or just as someone who wants to become a better person, success will require patience and perseverance.

We can achieve and demonstrate perseverance in many (and sometimes small) ways. The other day I sat in the sauna and was determined to sit for the full amount of time in the hourglass, so I persevered. I know that being in a sauna has many benefits, and that day I wanted to stay as long as I could, relaxing and meditating. It was not easy as I am not very good with too much heat, but I slept like a baby that night. I persevered with something small, and was very pleased with my achievement.

I did not grow up with parents who had a lot of patience. Life was not easy for them, and they wanted me to be seen and not heard. I was expected to get on with things and achieve, not so much because they wanted me to achieve something, but rather because it made life so much easier for them. When I was tasked with something like assembling a shelf, for example, it would take me a bit longer to assemble it than my father thought necessary. Most often he stepped in, told me I was no good with my hands and did it himself. Overall, that served me well in life. Not only did I discover later on that I am very good with my hands (and not just for typing these lines), but I realized too what a big issue patience has always been in my life. All my life I wanted to change and improve myself; to achieve and succeed, but success did not always come easily.

I flunked my translator exam the first time I took it. After practising for another year, I passed with flying colours. A kind professor helped me with this, too. My translator exam was my first official failure, and I was acutely aware of it. However, this failure encouraged me to apply myself more thoroughly. I discovered perseverance: learning English each day, translating, listening, reading and memorizing vocabulary. I developed an attitude of perseverance that set me up for later in life, when other, bigger challenges came my way that demanded patience and perseverance. Did I always succeed? Of course not. I am sure that I lacked patience with my children, and I used to be very competitive at work, too. I wanted it *now*, easily and effortlessly, but I learned life is not that way. Life asked me for patience, over and over again, and to apply myself calmly and develop greater perseverance.

Someone once said that indefinite patience leads to immediate results. I truly believe that. But who has indefinite patience? Not in our world of instant gratification; of time limits; of being busy and stressed. With infinite patience our world would be very different. Imagine that! Patience with our children would allow them the time they need to develop the right skills at the right time. School might be less concerned with teaching a strict curriculum, but may also teach skills that are important for life: acceptance, applying ourselves and developing compassion and kindness to name just a few.

Many examples of success have also been examples of patience and perseverance. It has certainly been that way for me. We all have life lessons, and patience and perseverance are mine. My patience has increased enormously and I have expressed perseverance, but I suppose that the story will continue. In our pursuit of success we have the opportunity to develop these qualities. Success and patience/perseverance are mutually stimulating. As we want to achieve greater success, we need to develop more patience and perseverance. When we develop these qualities, we support, enable and underpin success in many ways. We will not give up easily, and are willing to attempt different approaches. We will pick ourselves up and try again. We become less hasty, and make more sensible decisions. Success, patience and perseverance are siblings – influencing each other, reminding us what is important and showing us where further work is needed.

Belief

Much has been said about belief and success, and many great books have been written, but allow me to share a few personal thoughts. Belief in yourself is the most important ingredient for success. I grew up in an emotionally impoverished environment. My parents were never told that they were loved, nor that they should believe in themselves. They were never paid compliments and encouraged, and, perpetuating what they had learned from their own childhoods, they brought me up the same way.

When I was nine years old, a young man in his thirties took an interest in me and taught me to play chess. At first my parents thought he might be a pervert, but then they realized he was not. As they were busy with their own lives, they were pleased that someone was taking an interest in me and spending the time with me that they did not have the opportunity to give. The man came from what was then Yugoslavia, and is now several independent countries. Whether he was lonely or had too much time on his hands I never asked, since I was a shy boy, but nine-year-olds do not tend to think about these issues and ask such questions anyway. I was just happy that he came round, taught and played chess with me.

I remember I did feel encouraged, and it seems that from there I started to believe that I was an intelligent person; someone who is able to learn and understand. My logic started to develop, and between the ages of 18 and 21, I played in a local chess team. In hindsight, I can see the value of having someone around me who believed in my ability to learn a game like chess. That encounter and time period sowed the seed of belief in myself. As John Ford, the car maker, so aptly said, "If you believe you can do it or not, you are right." Your own belief in yourself; in your talent and ability, is fundamental to your success.

Later on, belief became a more conscious issue in my life. Training and working with NLP and hypnotherapy was part of that journey. I explored how I could remove conscious and unconscious barriers to believing in myself. My self-defeating beliefs and commentary were but two examples. I used to punish myself with negative and polluted self-talk. As I started to consciously listen to my inner talk, I realized that I did not have to believe in what I told myself. My mind was just working from a position of programmed fears from childhood and reiterating what it was perceiving from a fearful world. I knew I was better than that. By changing my thoughts, I created different feelings too, and over time I was changing many of my beliefs. I opened up to a multitude of avenues. We can all do that when we use our heart and mind to start to work from a perspective of love, and in doing so we create more positive beliefs. We have a superb instrument, and our heart does lead the way.

Limiting beliefs tell us it cannot be done. There are, of course, a few areas where common sense confirms that. We will not become a superb athlete, or a heart surgeon, at the age of 60. Neither will life have taught us enough to be a philosopher at the age of 20 (perhaps with the odd exception here). We listen to our doubting mind too often, and we look at our world and see limits instead of possibilities. Spread your wings and fly! Challenge your limiting beliefs – this is a great start. Beliefs are formed by thoughts that we repeat very often. These thoughts become habitual, and over time, thoughts become beliefs. When we think in terms of limits, we create limiting beliefs. Our negative thoughts that have occurred very often imprint themselves onto our soul and mind, darkening our soul so that we shine less brightly, and they hold our mind a prisoner. We start to change our limiting beliefs when we challenge our thinking and ensuing feelings. This is a process that can be (but does not have to be) a long one. Sometimes a feeling – maybe from our past – leads to negative thinking, too. Challenge your thoughts and feelings and you will start a process of change.

We also create limiting beliefs by listening to gossip, and by indoctrinating ourselves through negative news. Often we react from fear and complain about life in many ways. We gossip about the problems in our world, and complain about our life. This way we confirm the notion of a world of lack and fear in our soul, heart and mind. In complaining about people, situations and events, we create fear within. In doing so strongly and regularly, we cause an inner sadness and depression. However, it is not the situations that make us unhappy and depressed but our indulgence in them; our gossiping and complaining about them.

It is not the situations and events as such that trigger, confirm and deepen our attitudes and beliefs, but whether and how we feel and think about them. Beliefs are created in different ways –

often, as mentioned here, through gossiping and complaining. Limiting beliefs are created over time, and frequently unconsciously. We start the process of changing them by bringing our conscious and unconscious thinking into the open; by paying attention to our thoughts and feelings and to our strong reactions and aversions, which often arise from our subconscious. There are indeed problems in our world and we do not want to be oblivious to them. We can acknowledge them but let them be, not giving them strength by focusing on them. We can focus our attention on beauty, love and possibilities, and with time, change our limiting view of this world and ourselves in it. It is when we truly no longer perceive ourselves as the person who bought into those many limitations that we change our limiting and negative beliefs for those based on love and opportunity. Then success comes, as we have become a totally different person.

Procrastination and Intuition

In our fast-paced world we will often feel pressurized to find quick solutions to our problems, especially in business. We mostly make decisions via our logical, conscious mind, as it provides instant access to our stored knowledge and experience. However, creative and innovative solutions to our problems often come when we procrastinate, not pushing ourselves to find instant solutions to the problems at hand. In doing so, we rely more strongly on our intuition, our subconscious or higher mind, and our soul to provide life-affirming solutions.

I remember the time when I was told I was being made redundant from my last sales job. Knowing that a good payoff was coming my way, I decided to take my time. I wanted to find out what the path ahead could look like for me. As usual, my logical and often busy mind was telling me to look for security; to save the money and find another sales job as soon as possible. However, another part within was asking me to rest; to just be and wait. I strongly felt I had to listen to my body, my intuitive mind and my spirit. I had been in a high-pressure sales job for a good number of years, and dealing with constant pressure had led to several physical complaints, therefore I was willing to give myself more time to decide what to do next.

It was on my first day of redundancy, while listening to my intuition, that I heard a clear voice inside asking me to write. "What about?" I asked, and was told to just open my laptop and write. So I did, and this is my fifth book so far. I have never looked back. While writing is not my only pursuit, it has become a strong part of my life. I allowed myself to procrastinate; to not make any quick decisions during my last weeks at work. As I waited and listened to my intuition, I received very clear guidance.

I encourage you not to rush ahead with many decisions, if you can, but to allow yourself to procrastinate. I have often heard that procrastination is detrimental to success, as it leads to idleness and laziness. This was the way I was brought up, but today I can truly smile about procrastination. Yes, sometimes we need not procrastinate, but to get on with life, taking quick action. At the same time, we can give ourselves permission to procrastinate on other occasions, especially when we are not sure where our paths could lead us. Sometimes a decision has to present itself naturally, and often these decisions result in a tremendous change in one's life. As Einstein said, his best ideas were those that came when he allowed himself to be; to dream and let go, not taking action at all. Procrastination can be a cornerstone of success.

Success – Small and Big

We often do not even notice success, because we have a certain expectation, idea or desire. However, we have the choice of reminding ourselves each day of success, small and big; we can start to notice success in small ways that ordinarily we might overlook, as our expectation is bound by the big picture.

Maybe we are able to make someone laugh, or we understand something technical we struggled with before. We might feel more motivated, or, after something did not work out the way we anticipated, we dust ourselves off and continue anyway, albeit perhaps in a different way. We might be able to take small steps in our business or endeavour, like finding further information or coming to terms with an unrealistic expectation, and we create the confidence within ourselves to take another step tomorrow – all these things being evidence of success. What prevents us from regarding these and other steps, insights and results as success? Perhaps it is our impatience, our unrealistic expectations, or our vision that is solely focused on the big results. Any and all of these factors can prevent us from recognizing and appreciating these little steps, insights and achievements as success. In the main, we fail to notice them as we do not regard them as success at all. Only in hindsight – and maybe years later – do we come to realize that all these little steps we took were steps to success; indeed, they embody success and were more than just steps towards it.

How can we see ourselves as successful if we do not appreciate these daily embodiments of success? By failing to do that, we can never see success on a daily basis. Luckily for us, we might become successful in any case and only realize in hindsight that these steps – the smaller achievements – were success already. On the other hand, if we do not see and appreciate all these 'small' successes, we might never feel successful, whatever we achieve. Or we may even keep success at bay, as lack of appreciation might prevent it. Through not seeing and appreciating, we negate our success. I encourage you to recognize, acknowledge and appreciate your daily successes. They might look small, but they can have a big impact. Take small but consistent action; work with the energy and motivation you have at any given moment, and you will create success.

Some of us have a view that encompasses a cooperative universe. When we ignore these small, daily achievements and manifestations of success; when we fail to recognize, appreciate and be grateful for them, we send the message to a benign and cooperative universe that we are not appreciating small successes and thus we are not worthy of it, and by feeling and thinking that way, we are not worthy of big and astounding success either. In being so, we focus on the lack and absence of success; we look, but do not see. As we fail to recognize any small success, we focus on a lack of success in our universe, and life and the universe respond accordingly by showing us and bringing confirmation of the lack we have created.

Attitude and Appreciation

A positive attitude and appreciation are vital ingredients for success. Successful people see themselves as successful. Most entrepreneurs have a mindset which says that "Success is mine, as long as I apply myself and work hard." We can succeed in many ways, and not just in business or in a job, but a positive attitude is one of the most important factors in that success. When we see our glass as half full, we pave the way to learning, growth and success.

Our attitude determines our life, not just our success. An attitude is a mindset – a way of behaving and feeling – that is shored up by certain values and beliefs. With a mindset that is open to learning and feedback from life; that shows determination and a willingness to develop patience and perseverance, we have a great chance of becoming successful. We create success by adopting an attitude that views life as an ongoing story, a story that allows us to change with feedback and apply lessons learned. An attitude that says we are prepared to be in it for the long game. Our attitude determines our behaviour, whereas our behaviour confirms and strengthens our attitude all the time.

An attitude of success is based on certain values and beliefs: values of hard work and the willingness to learn and expand, of excellence in communication and of acceptance of differences. Most of the time we achieve success together with other people who are our allies in success. A value of openness and excellent communication skills are part of potential success. We do need a belief, too, that success is possible; that striving for success is success in itself; that our willingness to change, learn, take positive steps and feel responsible for success and failure paves the way for success. If we do not believe we are successful and can continue to be so, success will be more difficult to achieve – certainly if we think we do not possess the qualities for success. A positive attitude is a very important factor for most of us. An attitude that sees the world as an unfolding story of opportunities; an attitude that impels us to greet each day as one of expansion and possibilities, independent of fearful messages from the media and others we might pay attention to. Opportunities do exist during more difficult times or recession; through debts and lethargy, too, and we can seize these opportunities with an attitude of success.

When we appreciate, we announce to the world and others how grateful we are. We cherish and thank life, people, circumstances and events. All of them provide opportunities for learning and growth. Appreciating small steps in our quest for success, we acknowledge results, changes and progress – as well as setbacks – that always offer us more learning. Our appreciation and our gratitude open the coffers of the universe: open up life. What we appreciate in a small way will also pave the way for success on a bigger scale.

How does that work in a simple way? Our appreciation and gratitude, accompanied by a big smile, do affect other people and their opinion of us. What we embrace, express and expand towards others – which are often the qualities we recognize in them, since they are mirrors of ourselves, too – will come back to us: a promotion; help; kind and friendly colleagues – the list is without limits. By appreciating others for who they are and how they deal with their challenges; by looking at their good points instead of focusing on the negative, we receive back similar energies. Who would want a sourpuss around them? We all like being surrounded by appreciative people and will, consciously or unconsciously, give back the energy we encounter. Attitude and appreciation are vital ingredients for success.

Second, Third and Fourth Chances

We often hear stories about individuals who started out with a great idea, set up a company, raised the capital and become successful overnight. Our media seems to be obsessed with trivia and celebrities, so we might form the impression from these things that success comes quickly to most people and companies. However, it may take a second, third or fourth attempt before we become successful with a business.

I had my first small business in Germany in the 1980s. A friend approached me and told me about an ex-prisoner who was bankrupt. Robert had robbed a bank as a 13-year-old and gave his father the money. He did not tell the police that his father had planned the robbery, was found guilty and went to juvenile prison. In prison he had a fight with someone who was subsequently killed by accident, which led him staying in prison for about 15 years. On his release he formed an idea for a business, but he needed 5,000 Deutschmark. I had the money in the bank as a student, so I thought about it and took the risk. We bought a big second-hand van and collected old furniture from the streets, which afterwards we sold in a small shop. All went very well. We found quality furniture cheaply, and by advertising a service that helped remove old and unwanted articles from households. We made astonishing profits. After a while, however, I realized that Robert was spending money like water. Each night he went to a local pub and invited other pub-goers to drink and eat freely, and he paid the bill. While Robert was generous, he was also spending our hard-earned money. I finally had to decide whether I wanted to continue in the business or to focus more on my studies at university. In the end, I asked my partner to just give me back my initial investment, which he did. Long story short: wrong partner, wrong time for a business.

Relocating to the UK after finishing my MA, I used my contacts within Nokia, where I used to teach English in Germany. Together with a local language school, I developed total-immersion English courses for the senior managers of Nokia, whose company language is English, and later extended this for Krupp and Thyssen. This business went well too, as we had a steady stream of students. They stayed in a B&B and improved their English considerably in weekly or fortnightly courses. At that time, however, I had already started to train as a hypnotherapist and planned to open a private clinic with my partner – later my wife. I released my share of the language business to my business partner who, so I understand, is still running the courses to this day. I established my third business with health products, and again I was able to develop it very well. This business provided a modest additional income for about six years. I closed it down when I divorced and had to focus on holding down a full-time permanent job in order to pay maintenance etc. I loved the products, but no longer had the time or motivation to pursue that business at the time.

I am now developing my fourth business, alongside writing and and temping, with modern technology: video emails, video conferencing, life broadcasting etc. – all great products which I also use to promote my writing career. This business has come at the right time, via the right person who introduced me to it. It is a very ethical network marketing business, with the right products that will also help me with what I want to do in the future. In addition, I have already learned valuable business lessons, like flexibility and forming long-term strategies. Dear reader, allow me a little product or business placement, if I may. If you should be interested in earning extra income, building a strong and potentially very profitable business with excellent products and an ethical company, you can go to any of my websites and the find the information there:

www.clausbockmannbooks.org

www.howtomanifestabundance.com

Many people have to start several businesses in their life and we can all learn from the feedback a business venture gives us. What do we need for success? I would say experience, the right motivation at the right time, a long-term view, patience and perseverance, among other factors. I would assume that many a business is successful because they are the product of the learning from a second, third or fourth attempt.

Certainty

Nothing in life is certain, and where success is concerned uncertainty is the only certainty. I remember how devastated I was at first when I failed my translator exam. I had worked hard and I was looking forward to receiving the qualification so I would be able to earn an income as a translator. In hindsight, I realize I had not worked hard enough. A few weeks after my 'failure' I told my professor at university and he agreed to help me with corrections and advice. He advised me to focus on the business market, working towards a qualification via the chamber of commerce with the aim of becoming a business translator.

Not only did I realize that I had a deep understanding of the business world and the language concerned,

I was also more familiar with the business language in both English and German. I passed the exam with flying colours after a few months. I learned, too, that developing style and beauty of language comes with experience of life. This is my fifth book, and each time I write a new book, my trust; my thoughts, wisdom, depth and style are improving.

I expect we would all like to have the surety that whatever we start will take off, and that we will pass with flying colours. Fortunately, and I use this word on purpose, we do fail: in our marriages; when our children do not all turn out to be model children; when we fail in a business or lose a job and have to deal with unemployment – all bring a great deal of uncertainty. Imagine that you could know your future in advance – for example, that your marriage is going to fail. Had I known my marriage would fail, I would not have married, but then I would not have learned the valuable lessons I hope I did learn. I would not be a writer today.

My doomed marriage tested all my qualities; my abilities were stretched to the limit and I 'wonderfully' failed. At that time I was not capable of expressing enough love, compassion and patience, among other qualities, to make my marriage work. After my separation and divorce, I had to take a very hard look at myself and my life. In my absolute devastation I came to realize that I had not looked at some shadow aspects within myself, nor did I have the right approach and attitude for success in my marriage. Fortunately I was able to work with forgiveness and letting go, thus later shifting aspects and trauma from my past. In the aftermath of my failed marriage, so I believe, I was able to develop new qualities that I did not know I possessed.

We all face uncertainty on a daily basis. We can only embrace this uncertainty as one of the certainties in the world. In doing so, we can connect with our inner joy and peace more strongly and effortlessly, and hopefully on a daily basis. In embracing uncertainty, we can revise our expectations. When we surrender to life – today; now; tomorrow – in each single day we will open up to a wonderment in life that otherwise is not obvious to us. We miss this wonderment when we deal in certainty, hope and expectation. Once we let go of the expectation of a certain outcome, we allow ourselves to be surprised by life unfolding. In embracing uncertainty we sharpen our mind and soften our heart – we become more attentive to the small and daily miracles of change and surprise that we might otherwise miss.

When we drop the expectation of certainty, someone can positively surprise us, as we did not pigeonhole her with our certainty. A sunrise or sunset moves us to tears; a neighbour's smile makes our day, as can someone thinking about us and sending a quick SMS – these and much more can provide meaning beyond expectations. Expecting and embracing uncertainty allows us to stay present to the simple and little things in life. This attitude helps us to make the most of life – certainty will never do the same for us. Once we embrace uncertainty, we start to shape an attitude of spontaneity and life does reward us in unexpected ways.

Be Your Best

"Just be your best." I have heard that often. What does it really mean, and how do we know that we are being or giving our best in any situation?

Being your best can mean many different things to different people. What I have heard often in this respect is to work hard. No surprise there, given the work ethics in many parts of the world. "Work hard and play hard" – how often have I heard that, in the UK and the US too? I have found that working hard is supposed to mean working long hours; doing overtime; being the first in and the last out. That does not necessarily mean that we work smart, though. In many sales jobs, for example, people are told to make a certain number of daily phone calls, thus generating enough leads to follow up. This is still the preferred way of generating business and achieving targets. Less thought is given as to how to go about this the right way; how to balance marketing and sales most appropriately; how to generate true interest. Sales managers still want to see, feel, and above all hear a buzz in the office as a result of many phone calls being made.

Maybe we can work in a smarter way, though, with more thought given to the task; with training, support and phone call aftercare being used, instead of just working hard. Working hard and being under immense pressure to achieve targets leads to frustration and burnout. Salespeople change jobs frequently, and cynicism abounds among colleagues. Of course, without doing enough, we will not achieve much. However, just working hard can be replaced by working smart, including working with care and love, looking after colleagues and employees with care and love, and by truly caring for the welfare of the customer. We create success by working with love and compassion, not just by putting in the hours.

Being our best is not just about working hard or smart, though. It is about discovering, developing and using character traits that, while they help us to become successful, also serve others, and which are of benefit not just to ourselves, our own success or the profits of a company. What are these traits? They will be different for each of us, but patience and perseverance, as mentioned here, are on my list. What about the willingness to be honest with ourselves, to be observant and self-adjusting in our behaviour and attitude; without harsh judgment, but with a gentle touch of love? Being honest with ourselves, we can truly observe and see our weaker qualities in order to improve them. It allows us to not hide or to overcompensate, for example, a lack of confidence through arrogance or bullishness. Being gentle with ourselves and others allows us to be clear as to what we might want to improve upon, while cherishing what we have achieved and become already.

How do we go about being our best? At the outset we set an intention. Within this intention we can be willing to learn and grow for our entire life, to work on our shadow aspects, to be open to genuine and loving feedback, to allow time for rest, introspection and healing, and to be ready to shed the skin of victimhood and become a more aware and responsible creator. How do we know we are doing our best? We know by the reaction we receive from other people. If we face resistance when talking to other people, we might be too rigid in our opinions, or need to improve our communication skills. If life is boring for us, we might need to challenge ourselves more. Friends might comment on our lack of engagement, or on our tendency to escape from life.

Life might not seem to go our way – we might be too rigid in our expectation and lack flexibility. When we are open to life, we see, feel and hear whether we are giving our best. Life, people, situations and events all provide feedback. Being and giving our best will change over time, and the more we develop our qualities, the more we will be able to be and give our best. The more we learn, grow and mature in intellectual, spiritual and love-based qualities, the more we can contribute. Someone in their twenties might give their best by being physically and emotionally strong; someone in their thirties might be stress-resistant and on an intellectual high; someone in their forties might be a great parent, developing patience and calmness; while someone in their seventies might be able to share serenity and wisdom. Giving and being our best is different for all of us, but without intention, it will not happen as strongly as it otherwise might.

Never Give Up?

"Never give up!" Another phrase I have heard often. We must show determination and perseverance to allow a business, job or project to unfold within the right amount of time. We never give up, and in this the right mixture of action, belief and trust is essential. "Never give up, as those who do will lose" is another phrase I have heard often, too. It seems to indicate that what whatever we do, as long as we persevere, are patient, take action and have belief, we will eventually be successful. Is that really so? Countless stories about successful businesspeople indicate that there is some truth in it. The owner of the company Honda, for example, was bombed out in the Second World War. He faced many difficulties which, had he given up, would have prevented the eventual success of the company. I know of several people whose stories have shown me that perseverance, patience, belief and an attitude of not giving up can certainly lead to success.

At the same time, however, does it make sense to regard an attitude of never giving up as a gospel? Do we stick to it no matter what? True, by not giving up we develop qualities we would not otherwise develop, and we underpin an attitude of 'can do'. We allow time for development, giving an endeavour, job or business the space to flourish. A job, business or project that takes time to thrive can help us to develop the qualities I have mentioned. Equally, in developing and expressing these qualities we create success. Still, we might not always be successful in terms of material results. Our business might not take off despite our efforts, we may not make any progress in our job or project, and all the patience and perseverance we have shown might not be making any difference.

Proponents of 'never give up' might say that there has not been enough action and determination, or that we have taken the wrong approach. However, the timing of the business might be wrong. We might be looking into the wrong area, or we may not possess enough of the right aptitude for this business or job, and our talents lie elsewhere. We might have chosen the wrong business; we do not have enough funds to keep going for longer; the job was precarious in the first place; the project did not receive enough support – in short, there can be a number of reasons why our job, business or project is not taking off. Rather than stubbornly sticking with it, we can use common sense. We have a good hard look at everything and might realize this is not for us after all. There is no shame in admitting something did not work, and we can change direction and readjust our path. It does not matter what we call it.

We can try again later, maybe with something different. The timing of the new job or business might be more appropriate; it might suit us better, or we might be better suited for it. In the meantime, we have learned from our 'failure' and feedback, have changed with it and matured in a way that allows our next endeavour to be more successful. With an attitude of 'never give up' we could waste time on something that is not right for us. Realizing that it is not is part of our learning and change. It makes sense to give an endeavour time to take off, but it makes as much sense to pack it in after not having achieved success within a certain time period. We never truly fail, but only learn and grow. Not giving up can be ill-advised, if seen dogmatically.

Coming Second

I once heard a US commentator talking about Olympic medals and saying that US athletes did not win a silver medal – they lost a gold medal. I was not surprised to hear such a comment from a citizen of a country that epitomizes competition. The US has become the most successful nation in the world by being extremely competitive. For them, coming second means being a loser, and has nothing to do with achieving, as only being the best seems to count. While that is a trifle exaggerated, we do seem to live in a competitive world where coming second (or third or fourth, for that matter) seems like losing; where winning a bronze medal and being the third best in the world seems to not mean enough.

I came second once in a German martial arts championship, and for a while I struggled with the fact that I did not come first. In hindsight, however, I am very pleased with this achievement. I was once told by some very competitive parents that school policies of encouraging pupils to enjoy just taking part, not necessarily to win, and to develop a team spirit were responsible for the UK failing to be a successful nation as a whole, and not just in sports. What kind of world do we live in where achievements, where doing one's best and enjoying whatever we do, is not enough anymore?

Success is in participating; in being chosen and asked to take part, or finding out what is right for us, independent of whether we excel at it or not. I remember one of my German students some years ago who enjoyed learning German but struggled with it. He was diagnosed with a condition somewhere on the autistic spectrum and overall, I felt he was very successful in having come as far as he did with his German. In our competitive world we tend to look at what we have not yet achieved; always striving to do and be better instead of acknowledging what we have achieved already.

I prefer to live in a world where coming second is seen as a true achievement, not as a loss. Our world of celebrating the winner only is a world where those who do not fit in are pushed to the sidelines. Competition means that only the best are cosseted, while losers – the old, infirm, disabled, troubled, or just those who come second – live in the shadows of our winners. Does that mean we should only pursue what we are good at, and how do we know what we are good at unless we attempt success in various ways? I remember doing some sports in the past that I did not excel at, and I have pursued some leisure activities, like dancing, that I enjoyed but did not excel at either.

Let us remember that if we support a world for winners, we can easily belong to the losers. The majority of us must uphold such a competitive world view, otherwise we would be living in a different world altogether. Feigning indifference does not help either. Unless we start encouraging each other to take up a sport, hobby, or even a job we enjoy but are not necessarily good at, we risk belonging to those who come second. Let's face it: there comes a time when all of us will come second. We might become older, get injured, lose our sharpness, become ill or go through a period of turbulence and bad luck. It is then that we might realize how lonely and fearful a competitive world is. If we do not want to live in a world where coming second is despised, we need to encourage a world of cooperation and participation, not competition.

Stepping Stones to Success

Every journey starts with a first step, and life and success are made of many single steps. Seeing success as a sequence of steps makes it palpable, doable and achievable. Sometimes an endeavour can seem daunting and we would give up easily, unless we achieved success a step at a time. Creating success a step at a time ensures we devote our best to each single step instead of watering down our efforts, as our thoughts and feelings are focused too much on the 'big result'.

Taking a step at a time allows us to prepare more thoroughly and to take time to consider the results. After each step we can see where it has led us. We might be nearer to, or further away from, our overall goal, but this step has been a success because it gave us insight. Instead of measuring success merely by results, we might want to consider measuring it by our learning from the process. If our step has taken us nearer to our overall goal, we are encouraged, and that successful step paves the way for the next one. We can congratulate ourselves in any case, whether our step has brought us nearer to, or further away, from our next step or overall goal. Each step requires courage, so just taking the step, independent of its outcome, is success already.

If our step has taken us further away from the 'bigger success' we have found out this fact. Therefore we can change, readjust and take our next step more deliberately, perhaps attempting a different avenue or approach. Creating success a step at a time takes away the pressure, too. We can relax and enjoy each step in the process towards success. We can allow more time and adjust our expectation, and in this, we set ourselves up for walking the path of success. We take action, evaluate both the result and the experience, and learn from them. I remember when I failed my translator exam the first time I took it. While I was devastated at first, in being open to life, an even better avenue came along. Later on, having focused on business translations with my diploma, I was able to set myself up more efficiently. I took a step at a time. The 'insightful failure' was of huge benefit to me.

A few months ago, I started a network marketing business with video email, which a good friend introduced me to. As I have done network marketing in the past (albeit with a health product then), I am open to this method of business. I have taken the usual steps, but so far the results have been limited. I take it a step at a time, though. By doing so, I can gauge what has worked and what has not. I am looking into different methods of marketing, both the ones recommended by the company and those that are not. I have taken another step via a different approach, and am giving this time to allow me more insight. Taking different steps has shown me an additional avenue for promoting this book, too. In network marketing, all-out and massive action is often recommended. Obviously this works for some people, but it is not for me.

I prefer to take a step at a time. In this way, I have learned about different methods which I can also apply to my career as a writer. All-out action does not sit right with me. It does work for other people, though, and this will sit right with their understanding, approach and attitude. Taking a step at a time helps me to breathe, observe and acknowledge, or to drop an approach. It takes away the pressure that accompanies quick and instant success via massive action. It allows me to find my own approach; one that suits me, while not ignoring other approaches either. It allows for learning, for adjustments, for different avenues and attitudes – overall, for 'my way'. Success is a path, not just a result. As Frankie says in his song, taking a step at a time is my way. It might not yield a quick result, but it sets me up for a much deeper success in life.

A Different Measure of Success

We shout success from the rooftops: stardom in music and films; financial success by fund managers; young entrepreneurs rising up quickly; success achieved by politicians or writers. As we live in a material world, this does not come as a surprise. However, there are other achievements that are not talked about as often, if they are seen as successes at all. This is success in terms of the qualities and traits of character we embrace, develop and express as a spiritual being in a human body.

Is it not success to live a life displaying compassion, kindness and acceptance, for example, when, directly or indirectly, we are bombarded with messages to be competitive, self-centred and proud? I remember what was common in my job in software sales: drinking and playing roulette after a successful quarter; the "I'm okay, buddy", "We've done well, have we not?" attitudes. It was not appropriate to admit softness, sensitivity or compassion as a man. Moreover, I remember a scene at work where I was under a great deal of pressure and buckled under the strain. When pushed by my boss, I started crying and that evoked a predictable response. I suppose I was considered to be not tough; not competitive enough. This was an extremely valuable experience as it encouraged me to write after being made redundant, and it certainly epitomized the kind of world I had been living in – competitive and somewhat cut-throat.

On the other hand, I have seen incredible acts of kindness and know of people who are doing a great job as parents, colleagues and friends. A good friend of mine is a fantastic parent, and I truly admire her for it. Success came with an attitude that says, "I do the best I can, and not just in terms of my job and career." We can do the best we can by acknowledging what we do not know, by allowing sensitivity, by developing compassion and by accepting others. This is success, too, and more so than just material success, prestige, fame and power.

One of the most difficult qualities to develop is the ability to accept life as is. It needs equanimity and patience, perseverance and trust. Developing these qualities is a lifelong process in which we refuse to give up; we remind ourselves often and we pick ourselves up when we have, yet again, slipped. True success is about being gentle on ourselves. Success can be expressed by living with a disability and enjoying life despite or because of it, or expressing compassion and kindness despite having grown up in a barren and soulless environment, devoid of love and physical affection. These are huge successes.

Success is about wanting to learn and develop, shoring up our belief in humanity, facing our own demons and shadow sides, accepting, embracing and loving them, and over time transmuting them into compassion, acceptance and serenity. Why do we not teach these qualities in school, instead of facts that we can find elsewhere anyway? We can take our life seriously in that we graduate from school having adopted values of tolerance, acceptance and kindness; by learning to overcome fear and obstacles, and by remembering and expressing who and what we are: love in action. Is that not a truer success than ephemeral conditions like prestige and influence? When we die, we do not take material possessions with us. Of course, there is nothing wrong with enjoying the material and emotional pleasures our life has to offer. After all, we are here to truly enjoy ourselves by exuding joy.

Success can be measured long-term. As much as we might value companies that have been around for a century or more; companies that have adapted to change, we can also value a life; an individual story of change on a personal level. Some people might have been angry, aggressive or aloof and unable to express their feelings, but could change and mellow to become more compassionate and kind. When I talked to my dad today, I realized how much he has changed in his 78 years on Earth. He had a very tough childhood, and became a miner who always struggled to express emotions. He was a person who told us to respect authority, work hard and be competitive, but he has become a much softer version of himself now. This is true success, and I told him so today.

When we teach our children to value compassion and acceptance, we create a different world. When they learn to see kindness as strength, and sharing and cooperation as normal, we create a different measure for success. Doing so; being so, we create a different world too: a world where personal success comes with forgiveness, with overcoming shadows and demons, with developing daily joy and finding peace within by accepting life and people as they are. We create a better world when we truly value these aspects and qualities of human living, alongside material success. In a world of 'success by a different measure' we can all live more easily and breathe a sigh of relief, and we can be who we are more easily – divine beings on a human journey that helps us to develop a successful life with and beyond material aspects.

Excuses

There is no excuse for any of us not to be successful, especially when we view success as a process of learning, growth and change. We can all see life as successful when we do not regard success simple as an end result that we can display as a trophy. Often, when dreaming about success – perhaps in business or in a career, with our studies or as parents – excuses stop us in our tracks. We may consider ourselves too old, that we have a handicap that keeps us from achieving, that we lack the right training, that we belong to the wrong class or that the world is just a competitive place and we cannot fit into it.

Numerous people have proven how success is possible against all odds. Such stories are well documented, and here I offer a personal one. In my twenties I met a young man at college who was in the process of learning to play the classical guitar. Everyone told him he was too old to learn this instrument, as most talented people start playing much earlier. He was advised that he would face an uphill struggle. While he took this on board to some extent, making his studies even more difficult, he practised for two or three hours a day for years. He worked so that he could afford good teachers to help him pass an entrance exam for a certain university, which he did. He soon realized, though, that his interest was deepening. After a semester or two of studying classical music, he changed to another university, where music was combined with psychology and cultural studies. He continued with his private lessons and practice, and later on, passed his exam with flying colours.

However, his interest in both psychology and music pushed him further, so he trained as a music therapist, which meant more years of studying. As he had already been a mature student, he was well into his thirties by the time he was looking for a job. Here again he was facing difficulties, as he was seen as being too old by some institutions. He moved to an area where hospitals employed musical therapists to help psychosomatic and cancer patients, and he has worked there ever since. My best friend, Dirk, still enjoys learning and changing. He taught himself to play other instruments, and uses them with his patients. They create music under his guidance, or listen to it – all part of a process of healing. While Dirk has been successful, he continues to be curious. Recently he taught himself the electric guitar, as well as African drums, and now he teaches people to play the drums as well. My dear friend is a total success. He is a true inspiration for me, and often when I feel I am struggling, I think of him. He has overcome prejudices and obstacles and I do admire him.

Other people like him can and do inspire us. They do not deal in excuses, and I am sure we all have people like this in our wider circle of friends and acquaintances. They provide the inspiration for us not to let excuses of any sort prevent us from becoming successful. Fire your excuses – you do not need them any longer! You do not need to limit yourself by using excuses, many of which have no basis in reality at all. By moving beyond excuses, we move beyond people's expectations. I come from a mining family. In my youth I was a civil servant with the German railway, and that seemed to meet the expectations my parents had for me. It was my father's ambition that his son would not work in the pits or as a manual labourer. For a while I lived a life that was, at best, temporary. Early on I realized – if only on a subconscious, soul-level at first – that my life was about expansion and growth. I went to college to do my A Levels at the age of 24, and on to university afterwards. It dawned on me then that I did not want to live my life according to what others thought might be best for me.

As other people have done, I dropped a potential excuse: that a miner's son could not be intelligent enough to be successful. I moved beyond excuses, and that has become a part of my life story. Having achieved intellectual success, I started looking into deeper, spiritual aspects of life, and my life has been a challenging and wonderful story ever since. There are no excuses, only opportunities. No teacher, parent or government can know what is best for us, when they say we are too old or too inflexible. Trust your inner voice and calling – they are your best advice. Pleasing others and living up to their expectations would mean losing control over our life. What makes us happy – what we need – is individual to each of us, so let us remind ourselves of that fact regularly. This is your life; you can live it to the fullest of your potential according to your own guidance – and you are not alone on that journey!

Success: Flexible and Fluid

The willow tree is one of my favourite trees. It bends easily with the wind; it starts greening early in the year and before other trees, thus gaining advantage from the season and growing more strongly. Its branches are smooth and it prefers to live near water, and this water intake, I would guess, makes it more flexible and fluid. We too can be like a willow, flexible and fluid, and become successful this way. Like a willow we can bend easily with the circumstances and times, and be alert to what is happening – we can adapt our behaviour and attitude. We can be flexible and change our values and beliefs, if necessary. We can adapt for success. Being like a willow makes success easier, not just in terms of material success, prestige and influence, but as a way of life: being flexible and fluid helps us to learn and grow more easily. It is the most flexible trees that survive a storm or hurricane, and when we bend with the challenges and problems in life, we too can ride our path of life more successfully.

In being bendy and flexible, we are able to give up resistance to change. Change is the only certainty. While many of us react to change easily, some of us might be lagging behind, but we can also anticipate and look forward to it. We can be ready for, welcome and embrace change. By going along with and embracing change with our flexibility, our journey from A to B becomes easier. We improve our life effortlessly, and adapt with joy so that all becomes a fluid process: we embrace change and follow our own bliss. Bending like a willow, embracing all, the universe opens doors where before we would have faced brick walls.

By remaining fluid we stay younger, too. Our body will age more slowly and our mind will stay flexible; we will not so easily become 'old folks' who struggle to keep up with the change of time. We will connect more easily to younger generations and become an example to follow, and combined with experience and wisdom our fluidity in life will allow us to be successful in many ways. We might become mentors to younger people, having learned flexibility, patience and perseverance. When we are flexible, we are able to see when we might have reached a cul-de-sac, and we can turn around to walk down another avenue.

Overall, our method might be outdated, or our attitude and knowledge need to change. When we bend like a willow, we are flexible enough to give up an endeavour when it is not going anywhere. We know that we might need to rest until we have gathered enough strength and momentum to carry on. We realize when we can only *be* and not do, as now might be the wrong time for any new project. Being flexible helps us to adapt on our journey of success, and being fluid helps us to weather any storm and glide through challenges more easily. It is the young and flexible trees that survive viruses and adapt to challenging environments where ingredients such as poor soil or a lack of light make it harder to grow. When we stay fluid and flexible we can overcome poor ingredients in our life too: we make up for a poor education by continuing to educate ourselves, and we balance a shadow of opportunity with patience and perseverance, attempting different ways and paths to success.

Our Attention

Each day, we decide many times where to direct our attention. We can choose to listen to fearful news from the media. In listening to stories of a world in turmoil; fears of recession, problems and disasters, we can become discouraged in our pursuit of success and excellence. As we listen to gossip and frightening news, we can easily stop in our tracks. We allow ourselves to be gripped by negativity, and this does influence our behaviour and attitude. A negative attitude arising from our fears encourages us to behave more anxiously. When our optimism and courage is under attack, we might achieve success less easily.

If, however, we focus on loving, positive thoughts and feelings, success will result as a by-product of them. It is our attention that determines how we shape our values and beliefs, and consequently, our success. When we attend to and look for positive news, events and people, we also focus our mind on success more easily. Our body language will be positive, and others will notice that, consciously or subconsciously. Hand on heart, do you not, like most of us, try to avoid a person driven by negativity? We might see a person with a grim face and a tense, stiff body and we are cautious, whereas we tend to gravitate towards someone with a smile on their face and a relaxed body; someone who is showing signs of ease.

When we focus on positive news, people and events, our resulting optimistic thoughts and feelings produce beneficial hormones within our body, thus in turn influencing our ongoing thoughts and emotions. With positive thoughts and emotions, our thinking is clearer and we are more focused, as we are not distracted by troubling thoughts, consciously or subconsciously. We are more resilient to problems, and we exude confidence.

Our creativity is enhanced – we are in the flow. As a writer, I can attest to these facts – whenever I allow my mind to worry, my emotions are adversely influenced and my writing does not flow at all. In such an instance, I have to distract myself for a while, acknowledge the negativity I have brought and/or created, and with conscious attention to my state and breathing, I quickly allow more positive thoughts to dominate.

We can distract and focus ourselves in many ways in order to regain joy and composure, which allows different approaches for different people: deep breathing and a focus on beauty, such as within nature; a rainbow or trees; calming sounds, like a relaxing CD; reading poetry or a chapter in an inspiring book; consciously remembering great times or people; reminding ourselves that we have been able to face and overcome many challenges. These ways and others allow us to find peace within once more. As we live in a material world, mostly determined by fear of recession, war, conflict, starvation and violence, we cannot completely escape negativity, and to expect this would be naïve. But while we cannot, and would not, ignore the world around us completely, we can nevertheless create a more benign world inside. We can do this now; today; this week – yes, *now*; *today* – when we have slipped.

Our attention helps us to create a more peaceful world within, and we do so when we focus upon the positive aspects of life. We achieve this when we nurture our body, mind and emotions with the right food, eating slowly and consciously, and when we avoid too much gossip, negative news or people.

Others judge us according to how they perceive us. If they see a relaxed, confident and kind person, they judge us more positively. Notwithstanding our talents, knowledge and attitude towards success in general, when others view us positively they will give us the benefit of the doubt when it comes to success. A potential employer, for example, will employ positive people more readily. Other people's positive perceptions of us open doors. Moreover, when focusing on love, kindness and success, we feel confident and muster the strength to persevere and be patient in difficult situations. Do we not draw positive events and situations into our life when we focus on thoughts of a positive world and life for ourselves? Without having to believe in a mirroring and benign universe reacting to our input either way, positively or negatively, success happens via people and their perceptions of and reactions to us.

Success in its Own Time

Success comes in its own time. We might not like that, and being impatient, we might rebel against it, but our impatience might hold us back. Indefinite patience yields immediate results, but who among us possesses indefinite patience? I believe that most of us have a part within ourselves that wants to take action, and it is better to listen to it, as it needs to be satisfied. Without it, in our impatient and active society, we might make ourselves even more restless.

At the same time, we can take action and let go of a specific expectation of an outcome. Success comes when we are ready for it; when life has taken its turns in the process to make it possible. It is not our job – not mine and not yours – to make success happen. It is our job to desire; to state our preference for success; to embrace, herald and enjoy it, but it is not our job to make it happen. Success might happen once we have learned more patience; to persevere and to show determination, or once we are able to express qualities within that shift our fearful perspective to a loving one. When loving qualities have engraved themselves within, they become a permanent expression of who we are. Success might just happen, because the time is right and because favourable circumstances are coming together.

It is not our job to make success happen. Allow the universe to express success on your behalf, when the time is right. The universe includes people we work with and who encourage, support and recommend us; benign circumstances or synchronicities; positive events and sudden shifts. It is our job to be ready; to go along with what is happening now even though we might not like it, and to truly accept what is happening right now, despite a seeming lack of success in the moment. Relax, be at ease – there is no hurry. What do we feel we are missing? It is this moment that makes all the difference. Many moments make an hour; a day; a life, and while being and doing in our life, we constantly change and shift life and ourselves. For most of us, personal shifts and those concerning success are gradual, but many shifts lead to huge changes and success over time. Success can come in gradual shifts or it can explode in any moment, because a certain momentum has been reached.

Relax and be – life is meant to be easy. Who says we all have to struggle and constantly strive? That is just another concept that creates fear.

Forget About It

Have you ever had the feeling that focusing on success too much might be counterproductive? Messages about success abound: we are to visualize, affirm and confirm our potential success; to work and play hard; to be focused and attentive; to have the right attitude and perspective; to form goals and work on our motivation; to break down objectives into chunks; to never give up and to be our best. In short: to be focused on success in every waking moment. Many of the above aspects have been mentioned here, too.

There comes a moment, though, when we want to forget about success. On the one hand, too great a focus on success and work makes Jack a dull boy, and yet we are here to laugh, love and live our joy. As we live in a material world, we are often told to be our best and apply ourselves, because only the best succeed. If we heed these messages, we tend to become stressed and overworked; our routines and habits dull our senses and the responsibility creates fear of losing through not being able to pay our bills etc. We forget to live and to be; to enjoy the moment and to express our love and kindness.

We become bogged down with all this, and we forget to play. For most of us it takes hard work to gain financial security, and having achieved it, we might worry about keeping the momentum up. We jeopardize success by focusing on it too strongly. Forget about success! Widen your concepts about success, too (refer back to the chapter *A Different Measure of Success*). We are successful when we are able to play; to be creative and experience joy with children and partners; when we love and are kind. When we see success in a narrow, mostly materialistic way, we trap ourselves and we become creatures of habit and routine, so boredom might set in. We are already successful when we are willing to apply ourselves, independent of our potential success. When we are willing to grow, learn and expand, not just materially, but also in terms of compassion, kindness and acceptance.

Success starts with our attention – we can set an intention to achieve success with our job, business or studies, but also in terms of loving qualities we can develop. Having set a strong intention and knowing we will do our best, whatever our best is in any given moment, we can let go. By doing so, we confirm our intention and trust to the world, ourselves and the universe. We are showing that we believe in ourselves and trust in a benign universe that will set in motion whatever is necessary. Set an intention and let go! Once done, go about your life, defocus, live your joy and just be yourself. If we are too obsessed with success, we send a message that we do not trust other people and the universe; we do not trust that we will be successful; we do not believe in ourselves – our obsession is a sign of doubt. The more we focus and visualize; confirm and work hard, the more we are telling ourselves that without doing all this, success is not going to happen.

However, we can stop trying to figure everything out and simply enjoy life. We are where we should be, even when we fail; when all is delayed; when we face blocks; when we become impatient and make ourselves frustrated; when seemingly adverse circumstances thwart success – still we can accept that all is well. Life is perfect, and it works out in absolute harmony. If success has not arrived yet, we might have to learn and change first; we might have to find a different avenue; to change direction. It is human to criticize and chastise ourselves, as we might not have achieved what we or others expect, but we are just living life. We are working through a fantastic play with colourful characters and surprising turns, never completely knowing what might come next. Knowing that all is well, that all is working out perfectly, we can let go, surrender and enjoy the game. Expectation can be replaced by curiosity and a sense of awe. We can be open to daily life and marvel at the way success works out or not. Once we apply ourselves and set a bold intention, we can let go. We forget about success and ride the path towards learning, change and success with utter joy and serenity. Try it!

Success and Courage

We do not achieve success without courage. Firstly, our courage shows in wanting to achieve success; in setting an intention. Many people prefer to be anonymous; not to stand out in any way. Recently, I met a very laid-back person who did not seem to care about anything in her life. "You see, Claus," she said, "if I decide to just not do anything with my life today, I will not starve. I will just go on benefits; do a bit of work on the side, and I could do that for the rest of my life. So why do I have to worry about money or a career?" Having achieved a safety net is a great achievement in our western world. However, it was never meant to maintain people for a longer period in life – just as a support while finding a job, to help for a while when we have fallen on hard times, or are sick, disabled etc.

Wanting to achieve success takes courage, as does planning success and setting a bold intention for it. We will be tested many times on our path towards success. We might fail, as I have done a few times in my life, or we might become disillusioned as our expectations have not been met. We will have to muster the strength within to dust ourselves off, get up and try again. Only courage can achieve that.

While we muster courage within to aim for success, we also develop qualities we would otherwise not develop at all, especially when we fail. We will need strength to try again; flexibility to try a different method, avenue or path; perseverance to keep going, and trust and faith to believe in our success, despite any setbacks. As successful parents we will have to work on our calmness; on kindness and being able to set definite boundaries; on our ability to see and foster opportunities for our children, and on helping them feel safe enough to explore the world they have been born into. When we go (or return) to university or attend training courses – for learning a new language, for example – we have to develop discipline and keep our mind fluid and fresh. We come home after a day's work, feel tired and would rather relax, but instead need to summon the strength to learn and continue for a while. We need courage to keep us from joining in social activities when we should be studying, and to sacrifice time and friendships to achieve further education.

I do not know anyone who is successful and has not shown courage. Courage can come in many forms. Sometimes we lower our standard of living for a while to have the means to go back to university; we have the courage to look after our offspring and be there for them despite often being sleep-deprived and lacking social contacts, or the courage to develop our mind and knowledge, even though we are immensely tired after work. Some time ago, a woman I had a date with asked me why I was developing a business and at the same time starting a career as a writer with limited outlook for success (well, thanks for that!) when I could just continue to work in software sales, earn a good income and enjoy good times; perhaps travelling and taking it easy. I smiled at that, knowing this would be my only date with her. What would I have wanted to say to her anyway?

Yes, it might be easier to stick to what we know and do – to watch football and go to parties; to have frequent breaks and holidays; to just continue with what is routine, instead of learning new things and developing ourselves. It might be easier to gossip and watch negative news, to accept we live in a 'rotten and fearful' world, or to just strive to keep up with the Joneses. We need great courage when we want success: as a parent or student, in a career or with a business or just in a pursuit of becoming a better human being. Strong courage is needed to swim against the flow of social life, and at the same time, to be bold enough to flow with life in general. We need courage to accept our life and setbacks; to desire to grow instead of taking the 'easier option', and to stick to our guns.

I admire those who have the courage to seek success. As a businesswoman or student; as a parent, dancer or singer; as a creative person or accountant – the examples are so many. This is not just about success in terms of material possessions, influence and prestige, although material rewards often result from our search for success. We also develop trust, faith and belief in ourselves, often shaped by failure, difficulties and disappointments. In our pursuit of success we have the opportunity to become better human beings by developing perseverance, kindness and compassion. We can see ourselves as part of a human family that strives for success – all in different ways, all with a common story; albeit on different paths, but all in the same boat.

That can mean to just be the best person we can be, in whatever we do. We achieve that by setting the intention for success and by being as present, attentive and vigilant as possible in order to notice where and when we stray from the path. Also by acknowledging the qualities we need to develop and to seek the courage and strength within; to keep going and by embracing our journey wholeheartedly, even if it looks, sounds and feels tough at present. We can be the best we can by expressing who we are with the deepest commitment from a perspective of soul and love. Success needs true courage, and I thank you all for seeking this courage within to stay true to your personal story.

Is There a Particular Way?

Is there a particular way to achieve success? Many books have been written about it, and consultants, trainers and experts have developed different avenues which they will claim will lead to success. Recently, some in my wider circle of friends have told me they are following and applying the 'law of attraction', having read the Abraham Hicks books or others on similar topics. While I believe this universal law to be true, I have not heard about many stories of success so far. In my experience, we often block ourselves unconsciously and need to remove barriers within in order to live this law effectively. Progress can be blocked by unconscious or unacknowledged beliefs of 'not being good enough' or other similar thoughts. We might still live and react from a perspective of fear, and not always aware of it, struggle to think, see and feel from a loving perspective that embraces success and abundance.

I met a person once who told me that he had entered life on Earth to experience and learn from poverty. His soul wanted to experience deprivation. Whether this is true or whether he formed this belief in life does not matter. If we see poverty as fate, unavoidable, noble or something we cannot escape from, our belief might determine our experience and our corresponding experience will confirm our belief once again.

If there were a unique path towards success, would we not all share or at least know about it? Or would 'the secret' be used only by some of us? Why do we not all apply the law with ease? While the laws of life are simple in some ways, they are complex in others. First of all, no one can take away our right to see our life as success. The path of success is multifaceted. Some have to work hard, keep their heads down, get on with it and reap the fruits of their labour at a later stage. I have had the pleasure of meeting people, often in sales, who worked hard and as a result were ultimately able to retire early. They paid off their mortgages and lived in relative security. At the same time, life can deal a surprise here, too. A job we thought was secure may be made redundant. We face uncertainty, maybe in our fifth decade of life, and struggle to find an adequate position as we are deemed too old.

While this can offer an opportunity for us to take stock and change our ways – realizing, perhaps, that success is temporary – some of us might struggle enormously. What truly counts is whether we are able to see our life as success. I, for one, do see my life as success, as I was able to change direction a few times: from a civil servant to becoming a mature student; from working with languages and becoming a therapist and healer to working in software sales; through testing myself by developing a few small businesses and by turning to writing upon redundancy. My particular story has encouraged, allowed and sometimes strongly necessitated change, especially when at a loss for understanding. I had to dig deep to find it. As I changed direction a good few times, I have had the opportunity, so I hope and trust, to develop humane qualities that we can all share in as human beings: deeper compassion and kindness; more patience and perseverance; acceptance and trust, and hopefully wisdom and inner peace. Most of all, challenges in life have asked me to be, embrace and extend the love I am; that we all are, and I trust that my friends will say that I do this.

Few of us have experienced instant success, but all of us have heard stories of it – maybe of a singer, actor or writer, some of whom are discovered and coveted. But is a story like this without challenges? Certainly not. We might encounter envy, have to deal with hangers-on, or discover how fickle success like this can be. In the end our particular song might become boring, or with time, we are considered too old, showing the wrong face for the current times. We realize that success can come and go, and that we can go from success and fame to relative obscurity.

Some of us work with a process of success more consciously and actively. Others let go or just enjoy life without too much thought and action. Some of us prefer to work on success in a material sense, wanting to feel safe and secure. Others look for success in a more metaphysical sense, wanting to develop serenity, peace and humility. Neither is right or wrong, but either can suit our particular story. For some of us, our story is shaped by an awareness of having a soul-contract that wants us to live a particular life. For others, life and success have been shaped by childhood experiences or close observation of life. In our ongoing story we closely shape success, sometimes opting in or out, according to where we are. We might take a career break, or have to deal with loss and death. Such things force us to take stock, and while we 'officially' take a recess from success, we may become successful in a less material way, as, for example, we may learn compassion.

There is no particular way for success. There is your and my way, at this moment in time. Being open to life, our way can change, sometimes radically and sometimes in a minute and subtle way. Life teaches us: there are many avenues to success and it gives us a deeper and more flexible sense of what success can mean for us. Books, teachers, experiences – all teach and remind us, but most of all, our life story is what we learn from. When we listen and adjust our ongoing story accordingly, we will always find our own – albeit temporary – path and method to attain success.

◈ Meaning, Love and Success ◈

Thank you very much for reading my book. Meaning, love and success, for many of us, may be the most important issues in life. While I hope you have enjoyed my little chapters about different aspects of meaning, love and success, they cannot cover every possible facet of such complex issues in life.

If we find meaning beyond material aspects, through walking a path of the heart, we can call ourselves blessed. Meaning can derive from just living a life that we pay attention to, instead of being lived by life. Meaning can come from little aspects: a positive attitude towards life and people; the intention to pay attention to daily life – the now – instead of mostly living in our past and future. We create meaning when we let go of a perspective of being a victim that might have created a belief that meaning could be found through pleasure and addiction. Instead we can choose to become a creator of our life; someone who is willing to serve life and spread love, creating meaning beyond our daily treadmill through working with a perspective of love instead of fear.

We create meaning, too, by exploring the many aspects of love in our life, with our family and friends, and through developing forgiveness and compassion. When we explore ourselves as the energy of love that we are, we create the biggest meaning. We create huge success indeed when living from a perspective of love – acknowledging, embracing and expressing the love we are. This is the epitome of success, outdoing by far any success we achieve in a material way.

Meaning, love and success are close siblings that go hand-in-hand. When we create positive meaning, we mainly walk a path of love instead of fear, and I believe that expressing the energy of love that we are is the deepest meaning we can aim for. Finding meaning by walking a path of love, we can never be unsuccessful, independent of how we compare ourselves to what is regarded as success. When walking a meaningful path with love, success in a mostly material sense loses some of its importance, and at the same time, success in a material way may well come to us anyway. The universe; God; the source is looking after us, and when walking a path of meaning and love, it looks after us even more – it is only our fear that holds the universe's benevolence at bay.

Walking a path of meaning, love and success is an individual story. While we walk it in concert with others; with the help of the universe, people and all there is, ultimately it is only us, ourselves, who can give meaning to our personal story. Join me in our individual and common story of creating meaning. Let us create meaning by embracing, expressing and expanding the love we are and assure each other that a life with meaning and love is a huge and wonderful success.

What is the meaning behind the desire to find meaning in our life? Why do we seek success and explore the energy of love we have and are? First of all, we create the meaning we give to our life. If we see ourselves as victims in life – for example, using drugs or living a life of pleasure-seeking – we fail to realize who we truly are: divine creators in a human body. However, we can start to remember and express who we truly are. For a while we might give meaning to our life as a victim, only to realize, having gone through this experience, that we are not victims at all. In seeking a life of external pleasure or experiences of altered states of consciousness through drugs, we can finally come to understand that we create more genuine experiences from within.

We create an altered state by focusing on the moment and breathing deeply; by being aware and listening to life in this very moment. In doing so, we might become aware, for example, of birds singing. Normally their songs might elude us as sounds of modern life drown them out, but we realize these birds are singing as an expression of joy in life. We are this joy, too, and birds just remind us, confirming to us who we are. Like birds, we are an expression of unconditional love and beauty. It is our choice to confirm that in our attitude, thoughts, feelings and actions.

In our search for meaning we seek out various (and often negative) forms of expression for a while. They serve to remind us that seeking more loving and beneficial forms of divine expression aid us better. Some of us choose a type of righteousness from among its many forms. I know of devoted Christians, Muslims and Jews who feel their view of creation, of how to live life and which values to embrace, is the correct and perhaps only one. Depending on the person, there might be a certain degree of tolerance, but rarely ever total acceptance of other beliefs. While on the surface it can look as if there is acceptance, its absence shows itself in little gestures and actions. A few years ago I met a devoted Christian, someone who is kind and compassionate in many ways, and I admire him for that. At the same time, he despises Muslims and people of other faiths, as he thinks and feels that they are totally misguided.

Righteousness, judgment, sneering – there are many forms of expression. All of us want to express and create, knowingly or subconsciously, whether from the fearful perspective of a strong ego or a more loving perspective from soul and heart. All expressions, whether positive or negative, are attempts to express divinity, even if misguided. All of us have been indoctrinated in some form: via religious beliefs, competitive upbringing or teachings of superiority in class, gender or culture. We feed our beliefs constantly, confirming them in our fearful behaviour – intolerance, gossip, righteousness, and by our unwillingness to look at our shadows and flaws. All it takes to start a process of letting go and moving from fear to love is our intention. Moreover, when we focus upon what all religions preach, even if hidden and misguided, we start to see the aims of our common journey: love, forgiveness and kindness. We discover our common divine qualities, and with time, are able to let go of our indoctrinations.

All avenues used to create meaning are divine expressions, and all are a path towards understanding who we truly are. For a while, we might focus solely on material aspects of human life. Often we become disillusioned, though, frequently by way of a personal crisis. A crisis can help us to remember, to recognize and to express and extend who we truly are: divine beings in human form. How so? By pursuing material success only, we play a game that instils fear within. We might feel that being competitive; being better than others, is the way to success. In this approach to life, our mind and heart is full of fear: the fear of failure, of needing to succeed and 'be secure'.

As we are focused on our own fear and insecurity, we ignore the plight of others. Their situation does not touch our heart, and we might think that if they just worked hard enough, they would succeed too. With our heart mostly closed, we are like hamsters on a wheel, feeling and thinking we might lose it all. We might be made redundant; we lose our health; we are becoming old; we cannot keep up; we lose our attractiveness to the opposite and same sex, and so much more – a life lived from a purely material perspective is hard. In the end, though, we might come to a point, having gone through these material experiences, when being tired, we ask deeper questions. We start to question our way of life. In a way, our soul, our spirit energy, finds a crack in our conditioned armour, and having come to a point of exhaustion, we are finally ready to listen to our inner voice.

Often this is a decisive period in life and we start to live in a more meaningful way. We ask questions as to why and how, and answers will come over time. Frequently, when we have pursued a life of success, we also arrive at failure. Failure, our feedback from life, helps us to change our ways. It makes us question what we have learned from our path of success. Failure can nurture great qualities like patience and perseverance. We come to understand that all we can do is to be our best. Our best can be to not just succeed, be focused and disciplined and to work hard, but to find compassion and kindness, too. We realize that never giving up can be a trap, and that letting go and changing direction can provide a deeper, more fulfilling path.

We might suffer traumas through our romantic relationships, even in our life lived from and with love. We might be cheated on by our partner; encounter loss and death; fail to connect with unconditional love. We may not see where love can and will take us; we can struggle with forgiveness and fail to extend our love beyond family and close friends. In this, we are truly blessed if and when we start to realize that we do not just have love within, but that we *are* the expression of love. Our path of love, whatever form it has taken, can and will lead us to an even deeper path of love.

We might have to understand and experience the frustrations of love first to truly connect with our soul and live more often from a divine, 'I Am' presence within. It is frequently when we have frustrated ourselves with love, having become tired, that we start to ask different questions. In asking questions about love, meaning and success, we connect with our deeper essence. We start living more joyfully and clear old conditioning. Step by step, we shed the millennia of fear from this life, from family patterns, from all incarnations (if we believe in them) and human history. By peeling off layers of fear, we come to a level of divinity that allows us to remember and recognize; to embrace, express and extend the love we truly are.

It may happen in small measures at first, illustrated by developing more tolerance; then by developing acceptance, while our heart is opening up more deeply all the time. We fulfil our destiny by living our life with purpose and meaning. In doing so, we connect with and express more unconditional love, as well as growing in kindness and compassion. Our long path on Earth has made us wiser, and this wisdom starts to guide us more frequently. We start to connect with success, too – a success beyond the material level. This is true success, as we express who we are. When we become and express the energy of love we are, we have found the deepest meaning possible, and this often goes hand-in-hand with material abundance. When we live from a divine perspective of love, we manifest material abundance more easily.

Knowing that we are just the guardian of any material possession, we are able to share material abundance more freely. We give of our abundance to others, and extend and share our money and compassion; our time and patience; our acceptance and embracing of otherness; our love and the willingness to be joy. We listen and are open; we learn and grow. We understand that our stories might be different, being at diverse stages on our journey. Some are steeped in fear, prejudice or violence; some are victims, having been beaten by life. They are still our brothers and sisters, and offer us the opportunity to listen, and to be and extend the love we are. There is no better or worse, just different; we are all members of the same divine family living a human life. Let us remember that all stories offer learning, and none of us is ever perfect. Let us embrace each other's stories and extend the love we are to all of mankind. This is the greatest gift you can give to mankind, but above all, to yourself. Thank you so much!